• When Song Is New •

When Song Is New

Understanding the Kingdom in the Psalms

by
RONALD B. ALLEN

THOMAS NELSON PUBLISHERS
Nashville • Camden • New York

Unless otherwise noted, all Scripture quotations are from The New King James Version. Copyright © 1979, 1980, 1982, Thomas Nelson, Inc., Publishers.

Scripture quotations noted NIV are from the Holy Bible: New International Version. Copyright © 1978 by the New York International Bible Society. Used by permission of Zondervan Bible Publishers.

Scripture quotations noted NASB are from the New American Standard Bible, © The Lockman Foundation 1960, 1962, 1963, 1968, 1971, 1972, 1973, 1975, 1977, and are used by permission.

Published in Nashville, Tennessee, by Thomas Nelson, Inc. and distributed in Canada by Lawson Falle, Ltd., Cambridge, Ontario.

Printed in the United States of America.

Library of Congress Cataloging in Publication Data

Allen, Ronald Barclay.
    When song is new.
    1. Bible. O.T. Psalms—Criticism, interpretation,
etc. 2. Bible. O.T. Psalms—Prophecies. I. Title.
BS1430.2.A36   1983   223'.206   83-8286
ISBN 0-8407-5825-1

To
• ROBERT BOISSEAU PAMPLIN, JR. •

Truly a friend who loves
at all times
(Proverbs 17:17)

Contents

Preface

This is a book on Bible prophecy . . . with a difference. It will contrast with other books whose Dewey decimal shoulders it rubs. The two distinctive features of this book are its roots and its intention. It is rooted in the Book of Psalms, and it is focused on the attitudes of the believer who lives in the age of expectation.

The Book of Psalms presents a great deal about biblical prophecy, end-time events, and the coming reign of the Lord Jesus Christ. But these old poems make these presentations in the context of music. Some of the Psalms we will discuss are obliquely prophetic; others seem to shout prophetic ideas. But the Psalms convey attitudes that range the gamut from deep distress to exultant joy.

In the Psalms we can hear the *music of prophecy*. This music is not all the same. Some of it is in a major key, some in a minor. Some is triumphant; some is despondent. But in the music of the Psalms we can develop a clearer picture of the concept of the return of the Lord Jesus Christ, a time *when song will be new*. May your song be renewed in the reading of this book.

Acknowledgments

Some of the studies in this book have been presented as lectures at several Christian schools. I wish to express my appreciation to these schools for the opportunities they have given me to prepare this manuscript. These schools include Western Bible College, Denver (September 1981); Multnomah School of the Bible (September 1981) and Western Conservative Baptist Seminary (October 1981), both of Portland, Oregon; Southwestern Bible College and Arizona College of Bible (February 1982), both of Phoenix; and Grace College of the Bible (October 1982), Omaha.

The Scripture text I have used in the preparation of these studies is that of The New King James Version (NKJV). Quotations from other translations of the Bible are labeled. On occasion I have presented my own translations from the Hebrew text to highlight an aspect of the original text more fully; such translations are presented for purposes of these studies only. At times I have used *Yahweh,* the biblical Hebrew name for God, usually rendered LORD (or Jehovah).

I wish to thank my wife, Beverly, and my mother, Vantoria, who helped me proof these pages during some very late nights. To Peter E. Gillquist and John Sloan, my strong appreciation!

As in *Praise! A Matter of Life and Breath,* I am particularly indebted to my family for the great lessons on the praise of God that are best learned in an intimate community.

May glory proceed to our great King.

R.B.A.
Advent, 1982
Damascus, Oregon

Prelude

Prophecy and Song

"But in prophecy,
where is the song?"

•CHAPTER 1•

A Prophetic Realignment

When you visit a Christian bookstore you probably take for granted the large displays of books on prophetic themes. Books on Bible prophecy seem to be everywhere. In recent decades these books have had a tremendous impact on the reading Christian public.

It is time we get our emphasis on biblical prophecy back on center!

Because of the explosive popularity of some of these books, they are now being stocked by "regular" bookstores. They are even in paperback racks in the supermarket. Books on Bible prophecy now rub shoulders with Robert Ludlum thrillers and the latest Harlequin romances!

Interest in biblical prophecy has extended to film. Full-length commercial films have been produced along prophetic lines, both by Christian filmmakers and by Hollywood producers. Major stars such as Orson Welles and Gregory Peck have presented the words of Revelation on film.

Prophetic Preoccupation

We may contrast the enormous interest in Bible prophecy today with a general disinterest in the subject just a century ago. When George N. H. Peters published his massive three-volume study on biblical prophecy one hundred years ago, it was hardly noticed. Today his work, *The Theocratic Kingdom,*[1] is required reading by serious students of Bible prophecy. But Peters was so obscure in his own lifetime that we do not even know the date of his death. In contrast, some of today's writers on prophetic themes have become so popular that one little girl was heard reciting, "Matthew, Mark, Lindsey, John. . . ."

Interest in biblical prophecy today is so high that the market is glutted. And some of the recent prophetic books are so garish in their design and outlandish in their scope that readers often call into question the whole concept of Bible prophecy. Some books are published with sensational titles, multicolored inks, nightmarish illustrations, questionable interpretations, and frightening dogmatism. Some of these books have presented dates for the return of Christ so near their publication dates, so as to preclude a second printing.

We are preoccupied with prophecy. We seem to be fascinated with signs and dates, chronology and detail. Some people read the newspaper wondering if today's new dictator is the beast of the Revelation or how the change on the Dow stock report might relate to end times or if the latest blow from Mount St. Helens is found in the Minor Prophets.

Somewhere we have lost what prophecy in the Bible is about.

Prophecy in the Bible is not really about the beast, the tribulation, nor about Arab oil. Prophecy in the Bible is really about the return of the Lord Jesus Christ to this earth with judgment and great blessing, and the establishment of His everlasting kingdom. Prophecy in the Bible exists not to satisfy our curiosity about the future nor to tickle our ears. Rather, prophecy is given to help

---

[1]George N. H. Peters, *The Theocratic Kingdom of our Lord Jesus, the Christ, as Covenanted in the Old Testament and Presented in the New Testament,* 3 vols. (Reprint ed., Grand Rapids: Kregel, 1952).

us: (1) order our lives so we will be prepared for the return of Christ, (2) live a life of praise in an unspiritual world, and (3) evangelize those about us.

Prophecy thus has three directions: (1) inward—we should be changed, (2) upward—God should be blessed, and (3) outward—people should be saved, discipled and energized to live for the One who is to come.

Reaction from the World

The very success of prophetic books has brought about an inevitable reaction. Some secularists, who have an incomplete understanding of the issues, have attempted to use prophetic issues to embarrass Bible believers.

I once had a discussion with a newspaper columnist who was interested in some remarks I had made supportive of the state of Israel. In the course of the interaction I sensed he had a strong interest in what I believe about biblical prophecy. But he had some misconceptions. In a series of articles in the *Oregonian* (April 1982), this columnist stated that Bible believers *desire* a war between the United States and Russia, as this war will fulfill prophecy and will help to bring about the return of Christ! Such, of course, is errant nonsense. While the writer did disassociate my name from that point of view, he *had* picked this idea up *somewhere*. Someone is putting things in such poor perspective that this newspaper man was constrained to write a series of articles warning the general public of the danger of Christians believing in biblical prophecies.

Reaction from the Church

Other reactions are coming from those who hold differing views of theology and interpretation. Not all of the teachers of the church, of course, believe in a future kingdom as presented in most of the current books on prophecy. We use the word *Millennium* (a thousand years) to describe the kingdom of Christ on earth. The word *premillennial* is used to describe the belief that Christ will return *before* the Millennium to establish His kingdom. Other views are termed *postmillennial* (Christ will return *after* the Millennium has been established) and *amillennial* (there is to be *no* literal one-thousand-year kingdom; the return of Christ will usher in the eternal state).

It is to be expected that the current enthusiasm for the return of Christ to establish His kingdom would be countered by teachers who espouse other interpretations. I have several books by churchmen of various persuasions written as direct responses to the premillennial presentation by Hal Lindsey, *The Late Great Planet Earth.*

Reaction from the Camp

More significant, perhaps, is a reaction that is coming from within the camp of premillenarians—those who interpret the Bible as teaching a future, glorious kingdom of Christ on earth. Some scholars who formerly held the premillennial approach have crossed over to an amillennial posture. Others are in the process of crossing over and describe their current positions as "agnostic" about anything more than the teaching that Christ will return. The reasons for these reactions vary with each individual, but may not the excesses of some prophecy speakers and writers have been a factor leading to changes in position?

Dwight Wilson, himself a premillennial writer, has produced a well-researched and somewhat angry book entitled *Armageddon Now!*[2] He shows that well-

---

[2]Dwight Wilson, *Armageddon Now! The Premillenarian Response to Russia and Israel Since 1917* (Grand Rapids: Baker, 1977).

meaning prophetic speakers and writers repeatedly have used erroneous interpretations of prophetic texts to frighten people into repentance or salvation. The use of "signs of the times" has been overdrawn by so many speakers that we weary of their excesses.[3]

We should not look for signs, but we should be aware of God's program. We should not measure people for beast's horns nor attempt to foist their names into the numerics of 666, but we should pray for the coming of the King, work for the salvation of the lost, and worship the Savior in our present lives.

Prophecy in Church History

In the Apostles' Creed we confess the faith of the universal church in Christ's return to earth to judge the living and the dead. The doctrine of the return of Christ is not new; it is as old as the church and is a central and basic teaching of the Scriptures.

C. S. Lewis was not known for his writings on prophetic themes, but he did insist on the importance of the doctrine of the return of Christ in an age of general indifference:

> There are many reasons why the modern Christian and even the modern theologian may hesitate to give to the doctrine of Christ's Second Coming that emphasis which was usually laid on it by our ancestors. Yet it seems to me impossible to retain in any recognizable form our belief in the Divinity of Christ and the truth of the Christian revelation while abandoning, or even persistently neglecting, the promised, and threatened, Return.[4]

---

[3]For further study of this abuse of Scripture see Earl D. Radmacher, "Signs of a Signless Event??" (Portland: Western Baptist Press, 1975). This is a reprint of an article originally published in *Moody Monthly* (May 1974) under the title "Signs of Confusion."

[4]C.S. Lewis, "The World's Last Night" (first published 1952), *The World's Last Night and Other Essays* (New York: Harcourt Brace Jovanovich, 1973), p. 93.

The only thing new about the teaching of the return of Christ is the level of interest Christian people have in this doctrine and the level of the debate generated by differing views concerning that teaching.

Before we develop the issues of this book, let us look at the general outline of biblical prophecy as it relates to the church and to the future.

I believe that the Bible presents in explicit terms the fact that when Christ returns to this earth He shall establish the kingdom promised in the Old Testament and confirmed in the New.

Isaiah's Grand Picture

The prophet Isaiah develops these ideas with vigor, strength, beauty, and imagery in chapter 11 of his magnificent book. From the stump of the felled tree of the House of Jesse (see Is. 6:13), the holy seed within that stump shall one day sprout as a Rod, as a beautiful Branch. Isaiah says,

> There shall come forth a Rod
> from the stem of Jesse,
> And a Branch shall grow
> out of his roots (Is. 11:1).

On this One will rest the plenitude of God's Spirit (v. 2), for He shall be the realization of all God's desire in man, fully exercising the demands of piety in the fear of the Lord. His rule will be *righteous*.

> His delight is in the fear of the LORD,
> And He shall not judge by the sight of His eyes,
> Nor decide by the hearing of His ears;
> But with righteousness He shall judge the poor,
> And decide with equity for the meek of the earth;
> He shall strike the earth with the rod of His mouth,
> And with the breath of His lips He shall slay the wicked.

Righteousness shall be the belt of His loins,
And faithfulness the belt of His waist (Is. 11:3–5).

Changes will come about in all of creation when the beautiful Branch comes to rule the earth. The picture Isaiah gives is of paradise regained. Carnivores will become herbivores; predators will lie with their prey; children will play without harm in the regions of serpents, for:

> They shall not hurt nor destroy
> in all My holy mountain,
> For the earth shall be full
> of the knowledge of the LORD
> As the waters cover the sea (Is. 11:9).

All of this will be made possible because:

> In that day there shall be a Root of Jesse,
> Who shall stand as a banner to the people;
> For the Gentiles shall seek Him,
> And His resting place shall be glorious (Is. 11:10).

All of this is consistent with the prophecy of the Holy Child with the fourfold name who shall rule on the throne of David forever, empowered by the zeal of Yahweh of hosts. Recall these familiar words of the prophet Isaiah:

> For unto us a Child is born,
> Unto us a Son is given;
> And the government will be upon His shoulder.
> And His name will be called
> Wonderful Counselor, Mighty God,
> Everlasting Father, Prince of Peace.
> Of the increase of His government and peace
> There will be no end.
> Upon the throne of David
>   and over His kingdom,

To order it and establish it with
  judgment and justice
From that time forward, even forever.
The zeal of the LORD of hosts will perform this (Is. 9:6–7,
  with punctuation change at "Wonderful, Counselor").

This grand picture of Isaiah is the goal of Bible prophecy: the rule of King Jesus over the earth in righteousness and majesty. As we have noted, we sometimes call His extended reign the "millennial" kingdom, from the Latin word for a thousand years (see Rev. 20:4–6). We should not think of the reign of Christ as having a time limitation, however. The "thousand years" serve to indicate an exceedingly long period of time, and the period ushers in eternity.

The Glorious Future

But between the Millennium and the beginning of eternal peace, Satan stirs up a final abortive revolt (see Rev. 20). He is soon cast into the lake of fire (see Rev. 20:10), and the glorious future kingdom expands and fills all eternity with glory, beauty, life, and light as God and His Christ dwell with His people forever.[5]

John prophesies:

And there shall be no more curse, but the throne of God and of the Lamb shall be in it, and His servants shall serve Him. They shall see His face, and His name shall be on their foreheads. And there shall be no night there: They need no lamp nor light of the sun, for the Lord God gives them light. And they shall reign forever and ever (Rev. 22:3–5).

---

[5]A complete outline of prophetic events is presented by Dr. Stanley A. Ellisen in his book, *Biography of a Great Planet* (Wheaton: Tyndale, 1975), "Appendix: A Chronology of End-Time Events," pp. 249–260. Ellisen gives full biblical data for each of these elements in the chapters of his presentation.

This is what Bible prophecy is about. Our interest in the beast and the bowls, our observation of the trumpets and the tribulation, our discussions of times and signs will be distorted if we lose sight of the Holy One and His reign. The events and personages which lead to the rule of Christ are not unimportant, but they must not be allowed to distract us from Christ.

A friend of mine observed that some of our current interest in the details of prophecy can be likened to the excessive attention to detail that sometimes is displayed in a society wedding. There appears to be so much attention given to details of the wedding that the *marriage* becomes secondary. Prophecy is about the fact that the eternal kingdom of God is coming. No squabbles over details should obscure this! Our very familiarity with the details of the prophetic passages may lead us to our ruin.

Did you know that we may not allow even an angel of God to obscure our view of Christ? When the great prophet John had seen the vast panorama of biblical prophecy, he fell down to worship at the feet of the angel who had shown him things to come (see Rev. 22:8). But the angel would have none of that, for he too was a creature of the King. So the angel said to the prostrate prophet, "Worship God!" (Rev. 22:9). Nothing is to stand between us and God, not the beast of the earth nor an angel of heaven.

Let's Hear the Music

Let us explore biblical prophecy in the context of the music of the Psalms. In this way we shall not only learn facts in God's prophetic program, but we shall experience attitudes and perspectives as well. And we shall concentrate on the person of God the Father and His Christ. Let's hear the music!

CHAPTER 2

Prophecy and Psalms

But where is the song? When you think of biblical prophecy, what do you think of first?

Do you think of elaborate charts and tables? Do you think of ghastly creatures and horrid images? Does the phrase "biblical prophecy" cause you to think of the books of Daniel and Revelation or of the popular writers on prophetic themes? Does the word "prophecy" make you think of Armageddon? Of 666? Of the beast and his prophet? Of the common market and communism? Of war and famine? Of judgment and despair?

Does the phrase "biblical prophecy" make you think of *music and song*?

The New Song

"Of song?" you ask. That's right! Among many other associations you may have concerning biblical prophecy, one that is essential is the association of *song*. A significant aspect of biblical prophecy is *the new song* that will animate God's creation and fill His people when the promises of Jesus and His kingdom are realized on earth.

Not only will music and song be a part of the kingdom that is to come, but also some of the great prophecies of that kingdom are themselves given *in song*. Somewhat unexpectedly, we find major texts on biblical prophecy in the Book of Psalms. As Psalms, these texts are musical settings. Here I am not thinking so much of the Messianic Psalms, as they are usually described. Instead, I have in mind those Psalms which speak of the *rule* or reign of God, both in the present and in the future kingdom. Many of these Psalms, in fact, have the expression "the Lord reigns." A common—and very appropriate— designation for these Psalms is "the Royal Psalms."

We've Lost the Music

When was the last time you heard a prophetic message that spoke of the music and song of the kingdom of Christ? We often find ourselves so taken up with details of interpretation, debates about chronology, and decisions respecting figures of speech that we seem to be quite unaware of the *music* of biblical prophecy. In many of the Psalms of the Hebrew Scriptures we have prophecy and music together. This is music we need to hear.

Some of the music of these prophetic Psalms is in a major key, with strong rhythms and bold themes. These Psalms include 98, 93, and 99. Prophecy, in other words, is a major theme.

There is also a music of the prophetic Psalms that is in a minor key and is unexpected and unpredictable, lamentive but still expectant. Examples include Psalms 10, 60, and 14.

We shall also find that there is a biblical music of prophecy that is martial and strident, with harsh harmonies—all drums and brass. Here we shall look at Psalms 2, 97, and 110.

Further, we shall find a prophetic music that is truly majestic, genuinely beautiful and fulfilling—with which the universe will one day resound. A splendid example is the Psalm found in Isaiah 12. These varied musical experiences should be shared by us all.

As we read and study these varied Psalms we will look for their message as well as their mood, for information as well as for attitude. We will listen to the *music*.

Back to the Psalms

As we think of biblical prophecy in the Psalms, there are two impressions we should avoid. One danger is for us to expect too much. The Psalms, for example, have nothing specific to say concerning the identification of the beast in Revelation. Nor do the Psalms say anything respecting the dating sequence of the rapture and the tribulation. Most certainly, the Psalms do not pinpoint the date of the return of the Lord.

Another danger in reading the Psalms for prophecy is to expect too little. For the Psalms do present considerable detail respecting the coming of God's kingdom on earth, the battle of Armageddon, and the glory of the King who is to come. In addition, the Psalms have an uncanny ability to present the tensions believers face as they live in the age of expectancy—for example, the onslaught of the enemies of God versus His righteousness.

Let me say it as boldly and plainly as I know how. It is time we get our hope in the Second Coming of Christ fastened into our *worship and adoration* of the Triune God. Prophecy is not given as brain food for a speculative head trip where dazzling facts are assembled for a gnostic astroprojection into the events of the future. Instead, the prophetic word calls us to worship God for His promised salvation, and to live holy lives.

Hymnic Distinctives

As we begin to think of prophecy in the Psalms, we are reminded of the distinctives of this part of our Bible.[1]

------

[1]Considerable space was given to this discussion in the first half of my book *Praise! A Matter of Life and Breath* (Nashville: Thomas Nelson, 1980), chs. 1–7.

The Psalms are poetry. It is not sufficient merely to give assent to the poetic character of the Psalms for them to have their way in us. We need to *read* the Psalms as poems (and I encourage you to read them aloud in your personal daily worship). In these poems of the Bible we find many of the conventions of secular poetry. An Italian sonnet and a Japanese haiku share a poetic spirit with a Hebrew Psalm. But the Psalms of the Bible are distinct in form and in image, in theology and in purpose.

The material form of the biblical poems is termed *parallelism.* Statement is followed by restatement, and these elements are to be heard together as they enhance one another. Read the following lines from the intensely prophetic Psalm 24 and see how this works.

> The earth is the LORD's, and all its fullness,
> The world and those who dwell therein (v. 1).
>
> Who may ascend into the hill of the LORD?
> Or who may stand in His holy place? (v. 3).
>
> Lift up your heads, O you gates!
> And be lifted up, you everlasting doors!
> And the King of Glory shall come in (v. 7).
>
> Who is this King of glory?
> The LORD strong and mighty,
> The LORD mighty in battle (v. 8).

I like to compare the poetry of the Bible to music heard through a stereophonic music system. The sounds of one speaker blend with and enhance the sounds of the other speaker. Condensed editions of the Scriptures often cut parallel lines. One should no more think of dropping a parallel line of Hebrew poetry than one would think of shutting off one channel of a stereo recording. We should listen to the two lines together in the same way that we listen to the two tracks of stereo music. The words of one line play with the words of the other to create an impression that is grander than either statement alone.

As we approach a poem in the Bible, we should not atomize the poem by looking at each verse as an individual unit. The poems of the Bible are written in movements or strophes, sections that correspond to a paragraph of prose. In the shorter Psalms we often find two, three, or four movements; some have considerably more. Some Psalms have obvious markers for these movements; in others the movements are more subtle. But we should look for internal indicators of structure as significant interpretive keys to the poet's idea.

In the poems of the Bible we find imagery that is distinctive to the Old Testament world. Some of the imagery in the Bible is transparent and common to world literature. Pastoral imagery is not limited by time. But some of the poems in the Bible use images that need to be explained to the modern reader, as they are based on cultural issues that were distinctive to a given time and place.

We shall speak much of the Canaanite concept of Baal, for example, for the poets of the Bible took particular delight in using figures of speech from Canaanite poetry which they then applied to Yahweh, God of Israel. In this way they both glorified God and debunked Baal.

The most important gain for us in learning to recognize the poetic cast of the Psalms is to be prepared to *experience* what these poems present. Poetry is the most compressed form of literature, and—when read correctly—may be experienced the most keenly. We do not just hunt for a message in the Psalms; we are moved by the Psalms as we learn to experience the message that they describe.

The Psalms are music. Not only are the Psalms recognized as poetry, they are viewed as music. They are Hebrew songs of worship and praise. These old poems which we now read and study were once the lyrics of songs. Many people still sing them. Some Christians sing the Psalms in the musical settings established early in the Reformation. One communion, for example, sings the Psalms exclusively in English metrical patterns set to Genevan hymn tunes. Others sing these songs in musical settings that are very new and contemporary. Maranatha! Music has produced an album of Psalms in the idiom of contemporary praise music.[2] Some talented musicians in the church sing the Psalms in extemporaneous song; many Jewish people sing the Psalms in traditional chants.

But however they are used, the Psalms beg to be sung. *The Psalms are music.* And the fact that they are music directs us to the active admiration and adoration of the Lord. The Psalms were sung in the worship services in the temple in ancient Israel. The Psalms were sung in incantation by the early Christians in their worship meetings. The Psalms have been adapted to nearly every taste and style of music used by the church throughout its history. If we learn to sing these old songs we will find ourselves prompted to have the proper response to God as we live in an increasingly hostile age.

The Psalms are relevant. The Psalms are poems and they are music. They are also relevant. The Psalms do not exist to fulfill our prophetic curiosity. The Psalms are designed to relate to our everyday lives, even as they met the needs of the believers in ancient Israel. They speak to us where we are and as we are. They *live.*

Following a sermon, a speaker is sometimes told that he has made the Bible passage used in the message come alive. We understand the good intentions behind such

---

[2]*Psalms Alive* (Costa Mesa: Maranatha! Music, MM0097, 1982) was based in part on the hymnic ideas developed in *Praise!* The composers and writers were Tom Howard, Bill Batstone, and Dori Howard. Chuck Fromm developed the concepts of a worshiping community of singers and praisers united in adoring God by linking the old words of the Psalms with the new praise music idiom of the 1980s.

statements. But we strive to make a more accurate impression. The Bible *does live* (see Heb. 4:12); life is not something that we bestow upon it when we present it well. Rather, when one presents the message of the Bible in a relevant way, we allow the Bible to demonstrate the life that it has.

My beloved professor of homiletics (preaching), Dr. Haddon Robinson, used to tell us that it is a sin to bore people with the Word of God.

It should come as no surprise that the message of the text of Scripture is a living message. We should expect to see its life. When a speaker becomes an obstruction between the text and his listeners, the life of the Scriptures is hidden.

Of all the Old Testament books, the life of the Bible is seen most clearly in the Psalms. By learning to read the Psalms as poems and to appreciate them as music, we find that the Psalms demonstrate their life and relevance most clearly to the modern reader.

The Psalms are prophetic. Not all of the Psalms are centrally prophetic, and certainly not all of the Psalms are prophetic in the same way—but they *are* prophetic. Even the most casual reader of Psalm 110 must come to this conclusion.

Our Lord and His disciples were united in seeing the prophetic aspects of the Psalms of their ancestors. In the early preaching of the church witnessed by the Book of Acts, we find that the Psalms were used as readily as Isaiah and Joel as prophetic texts—and this despite the poetic and musical values we have already observed.[3]

At times Christ and His disciples seemed to go out of their way to stress the prophetic nature of the Psalms. Jesus quoted from Psalm 78 so that "it might be fulfilled

---

[3]Witness, for example, Peter's famed sermon on Pentecost (Acts 2:14–36) in which the apostle uses Psalm 16:8–11 and Psalm 110:1 with the same prophetic authority as he does Joel 2:28–32.

which was spoken by the prophet" (Matt. 13:35). The "prophet" here was the psalmist! Our Lord also spoke in reference to David's prophecy in Psalm 110 (see Matt. 22:43–46; Mark 12:35–37; Luke 20:41–44) and in Psalm 2. A characteristic apostolic opinion of the prophetic nature of the Psalms is found in Acts 4:25: "You spoke by the Holy Spirit through the mouth of your servant, our father David" (NIV).

In your reading of these pages, I trust that you will respond to the Psalms in a variety of ways. Since the Psalms are *poetry,* we should learn to experience this art more fully. Since the Psalms are *music,* we should allow the Psalms to aid us in our worship of the Lord together. Since the Psalms are *life-related,* we may apply the teachings of these poems to our own living. And since the Psalms are *prophetic,* we have ample warrant to study Bible prophecy as it is presented.

Some Cautions

There are some aspects of the study of biblical prophecy that call for caution on our part. For some reason, which I honestly do not understand, there often seems to be a great deal of private interpretation, even nuttiness, associated with the study of the prophetic Scriptures. This observation is not concerned exclusively with the study of the Psalms, but with prophecy in general.

The great book that concludes our Bible begins with a significant blessing to those who read it rightly: "Blessed is the one who reads the words of this prophecy, and blessed are those who hear it and take to heart what is written in it, because the time is near" (Rev. 1:3 NIV). Despite the promise of blessings one should expect in the study of biblical prophecy, there is the potential danger of a curse as well. The verse just quoted speaks not only of reading but also of hearing and taking to heart. Some seem only to read (and not very well), and then go out to deceive God's people with their errors. They make no adjustments in their lives by way of response to God's prophetic word. In my opinion, no part of the Scriptures has been so regularly abused as the prophetic portions.

Some cautions that we need to observe in our study of biblical prophecy are as follows:

Professionalism. As with any topic, biblical or secular, there is a danger of one becoming so familiar with the material that it ceases to make an impression on one's life. This is "professionalism" in a negative sense. This type of thing sometimes happens when a person begins his or her study with great enthusiasm. But in time the keen edge is lost; and the study of biblical prophecy becomes simply something one does, not something to which one relates.

Sensationalism. A second area for caution in the study of biblical prophecy concerns sensationalism. There are some speakers on prophetic themes who seem to feel that the only way they will get an audience is to shock their hearers with outrageous concepts. Just a few years ago, for example, there were those who were attempting to prove that the United States secretary of state bore a name with the numerical equivalent of the mysterious "666" of Revelation 13:18.[4]

Those of us who teach the Word of God ought to be alert to the potential of confusing our own foolishness with the words of Scripture. A reading of Revelation 13 presents a picture of the beast that is so evil that I find it hard to imagine how well-meaning men could be guilty of the terrible slander of asserting that a certain person is the beast. This practice may be a crowd-pleaser; it can hardly please the Lord.

Isolationism. Yet another danger in the study of the

---

[4]There is a whimsical note in *Eternity* (November 1982, p. 64) that shows that one can make any name total 666 to identify a potential antichrist.

prophetic Scriptures is to retreat from life—to leave both gainful employment and personal witness in order to "await" the second coming. Such an attitude seems to have been present from the time of the early church, and it is often observed today.

There are, by the way, even Jewish isolationists who await the coming of a messiah. The people who were responsible for the Dead Sea Scrolls were isolationists. They retreated from their society and prepared themselves for the advent of the age to come following the final battle. There are Jewish isolationists today as well. The Jewish inhabitants of Mea Shearim in Jerusalem have produced a Jewish ghetto in the holy city. They reject the present state of Israel because it was not established by the rule of the messiah, for whom they wait.

Among both Christians and Jews there are those who argue for a withdrawal from society and a denial of activity. Paul wrote to Christians with stern language:

> We hear that some among you are idle. They are not busy; they are busybodies. Such people we command and urge in the Lord Jesus Christ, to settle down and earn the bread they eat. And as for you, brothers, never tire of doing what is right (2 Thess. 3:11–13 NIV).

Martin Luther is reported to have said that if he *knew* that the return of the Lord were tomorrow, he would plant a tree today. As we anticipate the return of Christ, we should try to live useful lives until He comes.

Disobedience. A fourth danger in the study of biblical prophecy is disobedience. This is seen particularly with respect to dating the return of Christ. The Bible does present an active sense of anticipation; it is right to expect the return of Christ in one's lifetime. But it is not right to predict the date! It is in fact disobedience to Christ (see Matt. 24:36). To say that our Lord said only that we may not know the day or the hour, but that we may know the month, is sophistry unbecoming a servant of the Lord! If ever there was an application of Aesop's story of the mischievous shepherd boy who called, "Wolf! Wolf!" it is in those students of the prophetic Scriptures who shout "The Lord will return on Tuesday!"

Presumption. One more item calls for caution—it is the presumption that we know everything there is to know about biblical prophecy. If any study of the Bible ought to drive one to his or her knees in humility, it is the study of prophecy (Philippians 2:9–11 is a *prophetic text!*). Yet for some reason we tend to be stronger in our pronouncements respecting the interpretation of prophecy than in many other areas of theology—areas lacking the interpretive difficulties that prophecy presents.

At seminary I teach a course on the Dead Sea Scrolls. As we study some of the prophetic texts written by ancient Jewish commentators some students have inquired how those sectarians could speak with such certainty in their interpretations of difficult texts (interpretations that have been proved wrong by the passage of time). One student observed that the arrogant confidence some of us display in our reading of prophetic texts may lead to similar disappointment.

On with the Music

But enough of these negative elements. Music, maestro! Hear these verses, selected from one of the poems of the Bible that calls for a new song. As you read these words, note how the Psalm progresses in three movements. This poem calls for a new song among all peoples; it does so on the basis of the rule of the Lord and the keen anticipation that *He who is King is coming.*

Psalm 96

I. Oh, sing to the LORD *a new song!*
Sing to the LORD, all the earth.

Sing to the LORD, bless His name;
Proclaim the good news of His
   salvation from day to day.
Declare His glory among the nations,
His wonders among all peoples.
For the LORD is great
   and greatly to be praised;
He is to be feared above all gods.
For all the gods of the peoples are idols,
But the LORD made the heavens.
Honor and majesty are before Him;
Strength and beauty are in His sanctuary.

II. Give to the LORD,
   O kindreds of the peoples,
Give to the LORD glory and strength.
Give to the LORD the glory due His name;
Bring an offering,
   and come into His courts.
Oh, worship the LORD in the beauty of holiness!
Tremble before Him, all the earth.
Say among the nations,
   "The LORD reigns;
The world also is firmly established,
It shall not be moved;
He shall judge the peoples righteously."

III. Let the heavens rejoice,
   and let the earth be glad;
Let the sea roar, and all its fullness;
Let the field be joyful,
   and all that is in it.
Then all the trees of the woods
   will rejoice before the LORD.
For He is coming,
   for He is coming to judge the earth.
He shall judge the world with righteousness,
And the peoples with His truth (emphasis added).

All nations and peoples are called upon in this Psalm
to join in the *new song* of the Book of Psalms, a song of

joy before our King. This Psalm is an example of the Royal Psalms, as it centers on the rule of God: "Yahweh reigns!" God is king *now,* and He is the king *who is to come,* bringing righteous judgment to the earth. All people are to respond to Him, for He is the only God, the creator of all that is. All people are to praise Him, for glory is due His name.

In the reading of this Psalm, did you listen for the mood as well as for the message? Did you listen to the music? In the Royal Psalms of the Bible we find prophecy and music holding hands. Here we find the song.

First Movement

Our God Reigns

"Some of the music in these
prophetic Psalms is in a major
key, with strong rhythms and
bold themes. These Psalms include
98, 93, and 99."

CHAPTER 3

Joy to the World

Psalm 98

> Joy to the world
> the Lord has come,
> Let earth receive her King!
>
> —Isaac Watts

We now begin the first movement of our study of prophecy in the Book of Psalms. We will look at three poems from the hymnal of Israel that speak of *the rule of God*. Psalm 98 speaks of the rule of Christ that is to come in the future kingdom. Psalms 93 and 99 complement this by speaking of the rule of God in the present. The God who *is* king is the God who *is to come* as king.

Some of the words with which we are the most familiar contain the greatest surprises. We have just not listened closely enough to hear what they really say. So it is with one of our most familiar Christmas carols, "Joy to the World." Since we sing that song at Christmas time, we associate with it the Incarnation—the picture of heaven's Child with blessed Mary, set in an incongruous stable in a cave in Bethlehem.

But if we read the words of this carol with care, we find that there is little in it about baby and manger, and little implied of death and sin. What *is* proclaimed exultantly is the joy that comes to the world in the coming reign of King Jesus: "Let the earth receive her *King!*" And here is the thesis of this book: *Song will be new when Jesus reigns!* "Joy to the World" is a prophetic carol which anticipates the rule of Christ in the church and in the ages to come more than merely a celebration of the birth of the Child in Bethlehem.

A New Response

The words of the well-known carol "Joy to the World," set to the music of Handel, are in fact a reworking of the words of Psalm 98.[1] Psalm 98 calls for a new song for all of the earth and for all of God's people to adorn the coming of the King.

Psalm 98 is in three movements. In the first strophe we sing that *song will be new among God's people when final salvation is realized.* Here are the first three verses of our song.

> A Psalm.
>> Oh, sing to the LORD a new song!
>>> For He has done marvelous things;
>> His right hand and His holy arm have
>>> gained Him the victory.
>> The LORD has made known His
>> salvation;
>> His righteousness He has openly shown
>>> in the sight of the nations.
>> He has remembered His mercy and His
>> faithfulness to the house of Israel;
>> All the ends of the earth have seen the
>> salvation of our God (Ps. 98:1–3).

When the hymnists of Israel call for "a new song," they call for a new and adequate response to a new act of

---

[1]The triumph of the hymn in the English church through Isaac Watts is discussed by Harry Eskew and Hugh T. McElrath, *Sing With Understanding* (Nashville: Broadman, 1980), pp. 118–121.

God, or to an act of God newly realized by God's people.

In Psalm 33:3 a new song is prompted by a new realization of the Word and work of God. In Psalm 40:3 God's great deliverance of David is seen as a new action that prompts a new song. Psalm 96:1 calls for a new song based on the new strategy of world missions. Psalm 144:9 speaks of a new song in the context of God's new work in the house of King David. Isaiah 42:10 builds on the new and future acts of Yahweh as a warrior in its call for a new song.[2] Even in the Book of Revelation we have the phrase "a new song" in the new wonder of the Lamb who is worthy (Rev. 5:9).

The new song of Psalm 98 is the song of the establishment of the earthly reign of Jesus Christ the King.

With His Hand, with His Arm

Verse one of Psalm 98 arrests us with the word "marvelous," a term used to describe God's mighty acts of judgment and redemption. The salvation that God is about to establish will provide astonishment on the part of men and women.

We are also impressed in this verse by the terms of personal involvement on the part of the One bringing the salvation: "His right hand and His holy arm." These words are akin to the language of the Exodus. Moses and Miriam sang of God's personal power in the new song of salvation from Egypt: "Your right hand, O LORD,/ has become glorious in power;/ Your right hand, O LORD,/ has dashed the enemy in pieces" (Ex. 15:6; see also vv. 12, 16).

When we read in our passage of "His right hand" and "His holy arm," we have pictorial imagery of the personal involvement of God in effecting the new work of salvation that calls for a new song.

---

[2]This theme is developed in our study of Psalm 110 in Chapter 10.

To Bring Salvation

When we speak of "a new work of salvation" or "salvation in a final sense," we are likely to be misunderstood. These expressions are not intended to detract from the finality and full-sufficiency of the salvation accomplished by the Lord Jesus Christ in His first advent. Christ died on the cross as the fulfillment of all sacrifice, once for all, and forever "to do away with sin by the sacrifice of himself" (Heb. 9:26b, NIV).

We use the expression "a new work of salvation" as the writer to the Hebrews did. In the context of the full-sufficiency of Christ's sacrifice, Hebrews reads:

> Just as man is destined to die once, and after that to face judgment, so Christ was sacrificed once to take away the sins of many people; and he will appear a second time, not to bear sin, *but to bring salvation* to those who are waiting for him (Heb. 9:27–28 NIV, emphasis added).

In *The Expositor's Bible Commentary,* Australian scholar Leon Morris explains the issues of salvation accomplished and salvation to come in this text from Hebrews in this way:

> But this is not the whole story. Christ will come back a second time and then he will not be concerned with sin. The thought is that sin was dealt with finally at his first coming. There is nothing more that he should do. The second time he will come "to bring salvation." There is a sense in which salvation has been brought about by Christ's death. But there is another sense in which it will be brought to its consummation when he returns. Nothing is said about unbelievers. At this point the writer is concerned only with those who are Christ's. They "are waiting for him" where the verb *apekdechomai* expresses the eager looking for the Lord's coming so characteristic of the N.T.[3]

---

[3]Leon Morris, "Hebrews," *The Expositor's Bible Commentary,* ed. Frank E. Gaebelein, 12 vols. (Grand Rapids: Zondervan, 1978—), vol. 12, p. 93.

So it is with our Psalm. The salvation here spoken of is *made possible* by Christ's death and resurrection, but is *realized* at His appearing with great glory as King to an expectant people.

Room to Breathe

The key term in verses 1–3 of Psalm 98 is the word "salvation." It is found twice in these three verses.

The Hebrew language of the Psalms is imaginative and vivid. So we should not be surprised to find that the word "salvation" has a pictorial base. The underlying meaning of this word is, in today's vernacular, "room to breathe." The word "salvation" speaks of proper space for depth and breadth of living.

The use of such a term for "salvation" in the Old Testament might have originated in the incredibly crowded living conditions of that period. We in the West—with our suburban sprawl, our love of gardens, lawns, and patios—have a difficult time understanding the living conditions in Old Testament cities. Our Christian brethren in Asian cities like Singapore and Hong Kong more readily understand.

Perhaps you have visited Israel and have stood on the ruins of Jericho, the city captured and destroyed by Joshua as the first fruits of conquest (see Josh. 6). If so, perhaps you were as surprised as I was to learn that the walled city of Jericho encompassed only eight acres. I once told this to people in a rural area of southern Minnesota. One farmer came up to me afterward and said, "Eight acres! I have a tractor that won't even turn around in eight acres!"

The largest city in Canaan in Joshua's day was Hazor (see Josh. 11:1–15). This city, upper and lower tels combined, measured 180 acres. This is quite a bit larger than Jericho but very small compared to modern cities.

Yet thousands of people lived within these cities, or were in their protection in times of war. The cost and labor of building walls sufficiently tall and strong to withstand enemy armies, and the building of these walled cities on available heights (or tels) of habitation, worked together to make small, crowded cities.

In such a place there must have been a longing for "a city without walls," for such a city could only exist in peacetime (as suggested by Ezekiel 38:11, where the peace of unwalled cities was deceptive). There must have been many people who longed for a time when one could finally have room to breathe, a place without elbows everywhere. A pilgrim in the crowded streets of the Old City of Jerusalem may get this impression today.

Salvation, then, is *liberation*. Freedom. Space for righteous living. It is room for living fully and deeply in fellowship with Christ and His people. Metaphorically one can think of many constraints on life beyond that of city walls and crowds. Sin itself may be like cords and bonds that wrap and tie us, and constrain our living.

Then the Savior comes! With shears and cutters He slashes and cuts away the bonds. He bursts the cords and sets us free. And we breathe deeply and fully. Then we experience *salvation*—room for depth and breadth for living.

Cords and Bonds

The world and its cultures are marked by cords and bonds of constraint and binding. One day the Lord Jesus, the Savior King, will return to the earth, as both Psalm 98 and Hebrews 9:28 describe. He will bring about the final salvation for which His people eagerly await. God's space, as it were, will never again face enemy encroachment. *And then song will be new.*

Going Public

The salvation that the Savior will bring will not be done secretly or in private.

> Yahweh will make His salvation known,
> To the eyes of the nations He will reveal
> His righteousness[4] (Ps. 98:2, personal translation).

The salvation that God accomplished for Israel from Egypt was a *public* act and was made known throughout the Middle East. This was prophesied in Deuteronomy 2:25:

> This day I will begin to put the dread and fear of you upon the nations under the whole heaven, who shall hear the report of you, and shall tremble and be in anguish because of you.[5]

The salvation that God accomplished in the death of the Lord Jesus Christ was also a *public* act and is to be made known even "to the end of the earth" (Acts 1:8).[6]

The salvation that is coming in the return of King Jesus to this earth is also to be a *public* act, and all men and women will experience it for good or for ill. How misguided are those who speak of a "secret return of Christ" or of a "return of Christ in heaven."[7]

It is in the *return of Christ to the earth* that the presence of God will no longer be elusive, the dwelling of God will no longer be hidden, and the knowledge of God will no longer be rare (see Zech. 8:18–23). God's coming salvation will be known internationally; the coming of

---

[4]Mitchell Dahood uses "vindication" instead of "righteousness" in The Anchor Bible: Psalms, 3 vols. (Garden City, N.Y.: Doubleday, 1965–70), vol. 2, p. 364.

[5]Compare Exodus 23:27. Many readers of the Old Testament conclude that the Exodus was secretive.

[6]The early disciples were charged with turning the world upside down with their message (see Acts 17:6). Each generation is to do the same!

[7]The latter phrasing is a desperate attempt to save face in the light of chronological blunders made by those who have disregarded the clear teaching of our Lord that no one knows the date of His return (see Matt. 25:13).

Christ will be literally a global event. Every eye shall see; every knee shall bow.

Government Takeover

Not only will the return of Christ be a public act, it will also be a *political* act. It is specifically to fulfill God's promise (see 2 Pet. 3:9) to His people that Christ will come to establish His kingdom. God will set up permanently His own government. Psalm 98:3 reads:

> He remembers His loyal love
> even His utter faithfulness,
> to the house of Israel (personal translation).

The major theological reason that Bible believers are to befriend Israel the nation and Jewish people in general is that God has not relinquished His promise to His ancient covenant people. Jews are still the people of promise. They are the community of God's covenant. And for those who believe, their eventual destiny as a people who will experience God's grace is assured, "for the gifts and the calling of God are irrevocable" (Rom. 11:29, NASB).

This promise to Israel animates Psalm 98. Song will be new when Jesus reigns, for when Christ returns he will establish the kingdom promised of old to His people Israel.

Over All the Earth

"And heaven and nature sing!"

The second movement of Psalm 98 states that *song will be new over all the earth when Jesus reigns.*

> Shout joyfully to the LORD, all the earth;
> Break forth in song, rejoice, and sing praises.

Sing to the LORD with the harp,
With the harp and the sound of a psalm,
With trumpets and the sound of a horn;
Shout joyfully before the LORD, the King (Ps. 98:4–6).

In this impassioned appeal for music, we find ourselves in the central declaration of this Psalm. Song *will* be new when Jesus reigns. The verbs are exuberant imperatives that call for vocal and instrumental music of great joy and excitement. The *shofar,* or ram's horn, of ancient Jewish worship joins the trumpets and strings in passionate joy. To the obdurate question of the tone-deaf nonappreciator of music, "Why should there be music in worship?" comes the response, "Why are there Psalms in the Bible?"

Music and Worship

Music and worship are as strongly intertwined in biblical life and thought as are the two long worms in an old cartoon who were so twisted together that one head said to the other, "I've forgotten which is you and which is me!"

The term "worship" encompasses a larger category than the term "music"; but we can hardly envision worship that has no place for music. The call for music in this section is enlivened by the catch-phrase repetition of elements. A close study of the interplay of words in this section will allow the reader to hear the music of the text, as it calls for music in the worship of the King.

With Instrument and Voice

The instrumentation in this text is suggestive, not exhaustive. We do not need to recreate the ancient lyre nor learn to blow the shofar in our worship today, nor for that matter in the worship which is to come in the everlasting kingdom. God in His providence has allowed the development of many instruments to be used to His glory. Guitars join organs, reeds play along with synthesizers. But all of the instruments made by man will be used to accompany that made by God—the human voice. This passage points to a time when instruments and voices all over the earth will be caught up in music beyond our imagination to adore the great King Christ.

The King, the Lord

The high point of this second strophe of Psalm 98 is neither lyre nor shofar, neither singing nor trumpets. The climax of the passage is the fact that the King who is the Lord, Yahweh, is now in our midst in this future projection. God *is* King; His reign is eternal. God *is* King, holiness befits His house. In the future projection of Psalm 98, however, that holy eternal King is Jesus Christ on the throne of David. The perspective of this Psalm is prophetic. The vantage point of the poem is future. The kingdom of Christ is visualized on this earth, "and heaven and nature sing."

As we read these words in our Psalm, we may conclude that we have heard them before. And so we have. When Isaac Watts rephrased the words of Psalm 98 to write his immortal carol, "Joy to the World," it turns out that he was doing what the psalmist himself did. For Psalm 98 appears to be a poetic recasting of the prophecy of Isaiah 52:7–10. Many of the phrases of our Psalms relate to phrases of that great prophetic passage which begins,

> How beautiful upon the mountains
> Are the feet of him who brings good news (Is. 52:7).

We are familiar with these words because of the use the apostle Paul made of them in Romans 10:15 respecting the preaching of the gospel. As we look at these words in their context, however, we see how directly they speak of the second coming of the Lord Jesus Christ. For the climax of Psalm 98:6, "before the LORD, the King," is matched by, and grows out of, the climax of Isaiah 52:7, "Your God reigns!"

Beautiful Feet

Imagine yourself to be in one of those small congested cities we mentioned earlier in this chapter. High on the walls watchmen are stationed intermittently around the city. When there are rumors of war, the watchmen are alert and restless. The life of a watchman must have been ninety-nine percent boredom and one percent sheer terror. One watchman looks out. Far off in the distance between two hills, in the wadi system, he observes a runner. The watchman is now quite alert. He gazes intently at the runner, fearful of bad news, but hoping for good. As the runner draws nearer, the watchman is able to see that despite the runner's labored breathing, there is an expression of joy—not terror—on his face. Beautiful! Beautiful runner! Beautiful feet! When a runner brings you good news, even his dust-covered sandals are beautiful.

The runner approaches the city. At last a word can be heard from him. It is not the word of war, but is instead the most blessed word, *shalom*! Peace! Peace and prosperity, plenty and propriety. Things as they ought to be. Cosmos, not chaos. This is good news of happiness, and the announcement of salvation, of room to breathe, of depth and breadth for living.

Down with the walls! Away with the constraints! Burst the cords! Undo the bonds! God is here and God is King! And it is of Him we sing!

Isaiah's Song

With such words the prophet Isaiah pictures the watchmen singing together and leading the congregation of the city in jubilant song. For the Lord has acted. With His holy arm He has brought about final salvation. This is to be done in the sight of all nations; all the ends of the earth will know the salvation of our God.

See how well the Psalm has captured their mood, spirit, beauty, and wonder. Here are the words of Isaiah in full.

> How beautiful upon the mountains
> Are the feet of him who brings good news,
> Who proclaims peace,
> Who brings glad tidings of good things,
> Who proclaims salvation,
> Who says to Zion,
> *"Your God reigns!"*
> Your watchmen shall lift up their voices,
> With their voices they shall sing together;
> For they shall see eye to eye
> When the LORD brings back Zion,
> Break forth into joy, sing together,
> You waste places of Jerusalem!
> For the LORD has comforted His people,
> He has redeemed Jerusalem.
> The LORD has made bare His holy arm
> In the eyes of all the nations;
> And all the ends of the earth shall see
> The salvation of our God
> (Is. 52:7–10, emphasis added).

Isaac Watts is not the only one to set the words of Psalm 98 to music for the church. Another paraphraser of the words of Isaiah and Psalms was Thomas Kelly, a nineteenth-century hymnist. He celebrated the prophecy of the second coming this way:

> Hark! ten thousand harps and voices;
> Sound the note of praise above:
>   Jesus reigns, and heav'n rejoices—
>   Jesus reigns, the God of love:

See, He sits on yonder throne—
Jesus rules the world alone.
Alleluia! Alleluia! Alleluia!

All the earth will sing when Jesus reigns.

In All Creation

"Far as the curse is found."

We now come to the end of Psalm 98. In the third strophe we learn that *song will be new in all of creation when He comes.*

> Let the sea roar, and all its fullness,
> The world and those who dwell in it;
> Let the rivers clap their hands;
> Let the hills be joyful together before the LORD,
> For He is coming to judge the earth.
> With righteousness He shall judge the world,
> And the peoples with equity (Ps. 98:7–9).

He is coming. And His coming will set all creation to music. The effects upon nature presented by the return of the Lord Jesus Christ is a recurrent theme in the prophetic and the poetic Scriptures.[8]

In our pragmatic, workaday world, we often have little patience for poets who speak of clapping rivers or singing mountains. How will these acts get a nail driven or a cake made?

Figure and Meaning

Admittedly the language of the hills being alive with the sound of music is figurative language. But to say

---

[8]In *Praise! A Matter of Life and Breath* (Nashville: Nelson, 1980), I have developed the message of Psalm 65 along the lines, In the Year of His Goodness, Creation Will Sing (pp. 198–213).

that it is figurative is not to say that it is without meaning. Language that is figurative can represent something that is quite real.

Clapping rivers and singing mountains speak of the restoration of the world. It now groans, but will be set free (see Rom. 8:18–25) to adorn the glory of God, her resident King. And we know the clapping of human hands can be wonderfully expressive of praise.

On an occasion when I was preaching in a large church in Arizona, I observed from time to time the woman who was signing my words for the deaf as I was speaking. When I spoke of praise, the lovely sign for the word "praise" that she used was a clapping motion with her hands.

The singing and clapping of creation, whatever that entails, will be but a backdrop for the singing of God's people! He is coming to judge and to rule. His rule will be unlike that of any other, because righteousness and equity will be the hallmarks of His reign. No longer will wrong be on the throne. Never again will disparity rule or injustice prevail. We should expect creation to sing, given such a prospect.

Ecology and Environment

It is also possible to see in the words of a singing creation a major aspect of the rule of Christ as it affects the earth. The ecological disasters of modern living will be reversed; environmental crimes will be rectified. When Jesus' rule affects the earth, the silent springs of Rachel Carson's troubling writings will be silent no more. Lakes ruined by acid rain will teem with life; air fouled by pollution will be pure. Mountains and hills ravaged by man will again exult in the blessings of God. When the King comes, not only will He cleanse the hearts of man, He will also rejuvenate His land.[9]

Song will be new in all creation when Christ comes. Song can be new in our hearts today, as we anticipate His coming.

Sides of the North

Sometime back, I was guest professor at the Alaska Bible College in Glenallen, Alaska. Glenallen is a place loaded with "salvation" in the sense of "room to breathe." At the time that I visited this remote area there was no television station nor movie theater. You can understand, then, the excitement of the young people over the beauty of May, a month with long periods of light and blooming flowers, that was also the time of the graduation banquet.

After a good meal in a rustic restaurant, we saw the film *The Sound of Music*. There was no screen in the room, so a bedsheet was hung from the ceiling by tape. It fell down three times during the showing of the film. The projector may have been made before Bell ever met Howell, so thin did the music seem in that showing of a story in which music plays such an important role.

But we loved it! In a town with no theater and no Philadelphia Orchestra, even a faulty soundtrack and waving patterns of light on an unstable bedsheet were enjoyable.

But I wondered as I joined the college community that happy night: Is our own worship, at its very best, to be compared to seeing a film on a bedsheet! Think of what music and worship will be when we are in the presence of the King who is to come! Then the hills *will* be alive

---

[9]A prospect of future cleansing of mankind's assault on the earth is no more a license for continued assault than the promise of no more tears is a license for battery.

with the sound of music; the rivers will clap and the mountains will sing. But more importantly, we will sing! We will be caught up in our own new song of praise to the King of glory!

Song will be new when Jesus reigns. But it will only be new with you if you accept Him as your King here and now, today . . . before He comes.

·CHAPTER 4·

God Is King

Psalm 93

In our study of Psalm 98 we found ourselves in a song of the future, a poem that prophetically describes the new song that will be sung when the Lord Jesus Christ returns to the earth as King. But there is more to the new song of the King in the Psalms than the music of the future. The King who is to come *reigns now!*

In the Book of Psalms we have a beautiful *balance*—a balance too easily broken by us in our failure to see how one poem interplays with another. There is more to the concept of the divine rule than simply the future reign of King Jesus. In fact, the future reign of the Lord Jesus Christ is best seen in the continuum of the rule of God established at creation and exercised through all time.

Often, some of us who prize the doctrine of the return of Christ have been guilty of minimizing the present rule of God. For those of us who might do this, there is a remedy in the strong lines of Psalm 93. As we drink deeply of the cup of this Psalm we may become intoxicated with the wonder of the *ongoing rule of God.*

Here are the words of Psalm 93 in The New King James Bible. Note the presence of the word "is" as opposed to "will be."

> The LORD reigns,
>   He is clothed with majesty;
> The LORD is clothed,
> He has girded Himself with strength.

Surely the world is established,
   so that it cannot be moved.
Your throne is established from of old;
You are from everlasting.
The floods have lifted up, O LORD,
The floods have lifted up their voice;
The floods lift up their waves.
The LORD on high is mightier
Than the noise of many waters,
Than the mighty waves of the sea.
Your testimonies are very sure;
Holiness adorns Your house,
O LORD, forever.

Benji Has Puppies

How many times do we look at something but do not really see it! Last summer our family was driving north for a vacation in Canada. On the way we stayed with friends whose dog had a litter of puppies. We picked out one—a male we named Benji—and asked our friends to save him for us, as it would have been difficult taking a puppy on a trip. From our destination in Canada I flew on to the midwest, and my family returned to our home in the car. They picked up our new puppy on the way home.

Nine months later our son Bruce asked me, "Dad, why does Benji have nipples?" I was milking one of our goats at the time, and I explained again to him about mammals and milk, and that both males and females have nipples.

"But Daddy!" Bruce insisted. "Why are Benji's nipples so big?" I went and looked, and for the first time in months I saw!

"The reason that Benji has such large nipples, Bruce, is that 'he' is about to have a litter of puppies!" The dog we came home with was not the dog we picked out. Benji had nine puppies. Sometimes we look, but do not really see.

So it is with Psalm 93. A casual reading—even a general familiarity with it—may not be suffficient for us to understand this Psalm well.

A Song of the King

Psalm 93 begins with the words that are so important in prophetic song: "The LORD reigns"! But in Psalm 93 these words speak of a present reality more than they do of a future expectation. The point is that the Lord does reign now. The study of biblical prophecy is needed to balance our theology. When biblical prophecy is seen as part of the larger arena of biblical truth, our views of prophecy are more valid and convincing.

When we read the Royal Psalms and confront the recurring words, "the LORD reigns," we find in them three uses. Some passages speak of the eternal reign of God who is King because He is the creator of all that is. Other texts speak of a particular aspect of God's rule, which He sustains over His people as their Savior. Other poems specifically look forward to the magnificent reign of King Jesus in the kingdom to come.

This threefold approach to the reign of God in the texts of the Old Testament was observed some time ago by the eminent Fuller Seminary professor, the late George Eldon Ladd. He wrote:

This brief glimpse of the idea of God's kingship provides the outline for the entire Old Testament concept. While [1] God is King over all the earth, [2] he is in a special way the King of His people Israel. God's rule is therefore something realized in Israeli history. However, it is only partially and imperfectly realized. Therefore, [3] the prophets looked forward to a day when God's rule will be fully experienced, not by Israel alone, but by all the world.[1]

---

[1]George Eldon Ladd, *Jesus and the Kingdom: The Eschatology of Biblical Realism* (New York: Harper and Row, 1964), p. 42.

The Lord Reigns Now

In this chapter our discussion of Psalm 93 will be in the line of the first great declaration: *Our God reigns now!* Here again are the words of the first movement of Psalm 93:

> The LORD reigns,
> He is clothed with majesty;
> The LORD is clothed,
> He has girded Himself with strength.
> Surely the world is established,
>   so that it cannot be moved.
> Your throne is established from of old;
> You are from everlasting (vv. 1–2).

Clothed in Majesty

In these few words, chosen with skill and arranged with art, we are confronted with the ultimate reality of the rule of God. In broad, evocative strokes, the sublimity and majesty of our great King are presented. Majesty itself clothes Him. Strength is His binding cord. And these verities are not new and recent; they transcend time. The eternal One is eternal King.

Bible prophecy probably suffers the most from its friends. We recall the words, "What are these wounds . . . ," and hear the response, "Those with which I was wounded in the house of my friends" (Zech. 13:6). We have been guilty many times of stressing the coming rule of King Jesus so as practically to "dethrone" the present rule of our eternal King in the Christian church. He is head of the church today. He *is* King, whether we realize it or not. *Our God reigns* right this very moment.

There are other times, when the world without seems to be exploding or our world within seems to be crumbling, that we tend to doubt the rule of God altogether. In the face of these doubts come the resolute words of Psalm 93: *Our God reigns!*

Eternal Splendor

God reigns, and God alone reigns. The devil is active on earth only by divine permission, and his franchise here is, at best, temporary. The word order of the words "the LORD reigns" in the Hebrew text suggests the exclusive reign of God, a concept to be emphasized by the content of the Psalm as well. The importance of the present, exclusive reign of God is likely to be lost on us if we do not have an adequate impression of the culture in which these words were first written.

Three millennia ago Israel was surrounded by, and often infiltrated with, ideas of pagan mythology. The gods of the nations achieved kingship through battles or crafty machinations. These gods would rise and they would fall in a frighteningly uncertain world. The chaos of the pagan cultures contrasts sharply with the sublimity and calm serenity of Psalm 93: *Our God reigns!*

The pagan god Baal is the subtle foil used by the poet of this Psalm to magnify God. The Canaanite people who lived in the land before Israel, and whose ideas persisted and ultimately destroyed Israel, had a highly developed mythology and a wide-ranging pantheon. In order for us to understand the thrust of Psalm 93, we need to be familiar with the ideas of the Old Testament culture.

Baal Becomes King

According to the stories of the gods in Canaanite thought, the head of the gods was the great deity Il, the creator of many of the other gods. A younger god, a deity on the make if you will, was Baal. Baal knew that in his power play with Il he could not attack Il directly, which would be "deicide." Instead, this young god Baal attacked three lackeys of Il: Yamm, the sea god; Lotan, the sea monster deity; and Mot, the god of death.

In a tremendous battle, described in splendid poetry in

the texts from Ugarit,[2] Baal was the ultimate victor, although the details of the battle are still a matter for lively scholarly debate.[3]

The clear points to be made are these: Baal becomes king by force, cunning, and skill, and by ample help both in arms and allies. Baal's right to rule is ever-threatened by the resurgent deities of malevolence and destruction. The world continues to be in upheaval.

In contrast that is stunning, our Psalm depicts the God of reality as one who is King from of old. *He is the King whose splendor is from eternity.* Here is no young pup who will have his day, only later to be replaced when teeth are missing and breath is short. He is the eternal King. His rule guarantees His realm. The world will not be overturned as soon as a new deity takes control. The belt of strength will not be removed from Him by another. He is "belted with victory."[4]

God is the creator of all that exists. He rules by virtue of His creation. He has brought cosmos out of chaos, order out of disorder. As the Creator of all that exists, He controls all the forces of chaos. "Surely the world is established;/ so that it cannot be moved" (Ps. 93:1).

Unchallenged Stability

Not only is the Lord King whose splendor is from eternity (vv. 1–2), *He is also King whose stability is unchallenged* (vv. 3–4). Here are the words of the second strophe of the poem:

---

[2]The Ugaritic texts were discovered in northern Syria in 1929. An accessible English translation is to be found in James B. Pritchard, *The Ancient Near East: An Anthology of Texts and Pictures* (Princeton: Princeton Univ. Press, 1971), pp. 92–132.

[3]An analysis is given by Arvid S. Kapelrud, *Ras Shamra Discoveries and the Old Testament,* trans. by G. W. Anderson (Norman, Okla.: Univ. of Oklahoma Press, 1963).

[4]This rendering is given by Mitchell Dahood, The Anchor Bible: The Psalms, 3 vols. (Garden City, N.Y.: Doubleday, 1965–70), vol. 2, p. 339.

The floods have lifted up, O LORD,
The floods have lifted up their voice;
The floods lift up their waves.
The LORD on high is mightier
Than the noise of many waters,
Than the mighty waves of the sea (Ps. 93:3–4).

The sea never ceases to amaze us as we view vast, uncontrolled, surging and seething power in storm—often tranquil, but never docile or at rest. Quite a bit more is involved in this poem, however, than our natural responses to the ebb and flow of the sea.

Underlying these verses is the imagery of Baal's conflict with the waters when he established his rule and the repeated threats that imperil him. There was always the possibility that the waters Baal was thought to control might one day overstep their bonds, burst their constraints, and destroy the fragile order Baal had managed to achieve by force.

The Insolent Waters

With the raising of the voice of the insolent waters in verse 3,[5] there comes a renewed question: Even though the rule of God was established at the beginning of time, is it possible that it might be challenged today? The forces of evil ever seem to threaten the cosmos God has established.[6]

---

[5]The pattern of parallelism in verse 3 in the original is: verb—subject—vocative // verb—subject—object // verb—subject—object. This emphasis upon the verb and subject by repetition builds suspense. The address to God is in fright, and the varying objects build a strong image of impending doom.

[6]Bruce K. Waltke has presented the ancient Near Eastern mythological setting for the concept of a god of restraint doing battle with gods of disorder and the relationship that these ideas have to the poetic imagery of the Bible. See his *Creation and Chaos* (Portland: Western Baptist Press, 1974).

We are dealing here with more than just a poetic image. In our own day we may speak along these lines in a literal way, not just figuratively. The great nations of the earth have within their nuclear capacities the power to annihilate all of mankind. Our surmise is that the survivors of World War III will be among the most unfortunate of that day. One editorial cartoon described the results of a nuclear war by presenting drawings of two immense pits, one pair of eyes staring out of the darkness in the "winning" pit.

The assumption that the superpowers will never use such force against each other because of mutual fear of retaliation is now offset by the proliferation of nuclear weapons among nations without such "scruples." Whether you be pro-nuke, a-nuke, or anti-nuke, we are living in a whole new chapter of human history. It had better be that you have the Kingdom of God and it alone as your final hope!

The Unthinkable Becomes Thinkable

The nuclear club is no longer exclusive. The thought of globally visible crazies using such arms has made the unthinkable thinkable. The Falkland Islands, a scene of recent international conflict, serves as a foreshadowing of improbable settings for coming world conflict. A minor conflict has the possibility of leading to global conflagration. These are the insolent waters of our day. Psalm 93 speaks to our present age even more strongly than it spoke centuries ago to the sorely troubled peoples of the land of Judah.

ABC television's "Nightline" reported on a survey taken in New York to determine the vocational and marital attitudes of young people in their early to mid-teens. A number of questions centered on the expectations that these young people might have for their own lives when they reach the age of thirty-five.

The shocking results of the survey were found in the lack of specific responses. When probed, the students countered with the words that *they did not expect to live* to the age of thirty-five! So real in their perception was the risk of nuclear warfare that the attainment of the early middle years was not even a prospect for them. Imagine the incalculable effect of such thinking on the lives of these young people! We *do* have our insolent waters today.

Mightier Is He!

We go back to the words of Psalm 93 in our fearful new age and we see in them how the raging of the insolent waters affects us in our own day. We also read the balancing words of the incomparable power and might of God which are given in verse 4:

> The LORD on high is mightier
> Than the noise of many waters,
> Than the mighty waves of the sea.

Some Christians respond to the threat of the insolent waters (nuclear arms) by sounding a call for a strengthening of the nuclear forces of their own country. These people sincerely believe that a strong nuclear deterrent is the best possible protection against an arrogant antagonist.

It is likely that an increasing number of Christians will join the voices of those opposed to the increase of nuclear force in any country. These people will be equally sincere in believing that the madness has gone too far and must be halted before it is too late.

Certainly Christians need to think and act upon this issue—one of the most difficult moral issues of our age. Christians will differ in their conclusions, but they must not be complacent about the issue. Based on the teaching of Psalm 93 and its implications for our age, Christians have a perspective on the nuclear issue that those in the world will not understand. This is the same perspective that Israel was to have, and which would not have been understood by their neighbors either.

The clear teaching of Psalm 93 is that because God *is* King, the world will not be moved. For He is mightier than any contrary force or power.

In these affirmations, be assured that I am not calling for complacency. Instead, I am calling for a full-scale realignment of ultimate hope in the Kingdom of God. Set your bearings there. The threat of nuclear war and its aftermath is a threat as real for the Christian as for the non-Christian. We all have a stake in the survival of civilization on planet Earth.

But the words of Psalm 93 do call for perspective. As we enter more fully into the debate of what to do or not to do with nuclear arms, we should remember that Yahweh, the God of Israel, is still King—glorious, majestic, possessing all power and all strength.

No insolent water—of the active imagination of the ancients or the all-too-real devices of the moderns—is a threat to His rule. What nuclear power presents today, so the raging waters suggested yesterday. But *our God reigns!* The calm wording of verse 4 should serve to soothe our worries as it served to soothe the worries and tensions of those who lived in a more rustic, but no less terrifying, age.

He Is Mighty

He is mighty! In the recitation for the Passover, the *Haggadah,* there are many splendid things said about God to celebrate His saving wonders and His splendid perfection. But when all has been said, the songs have been sung, and the feast has been consumed, then comes the time for the prayer for divine acceptance of the Passover *Seder* (order). The last thing that is said is *'Adîr Hû'*, "mighty is He!"

The Hebrew word *'adîr* is used two times in Psalm 93:4, once in an intensive plural and once in the singular. Truly we may sing with the redeemed of all the ages and with all of God's holy angels: *'Adîr Hû'*, "mighty is He!"

Psalm 93 teaches that the Lord is King whose reign is from eternity (vv. 1–2), whose stability is unchallenged (vv. 3–4). The Psalm then concludes by saying that *Yahweh is King whose statutes endure forever* (v. 5). Hear now these words:

> Your testimonies are very sure;
> Holiness adorns Your house,
> O LORD, forever (Ps. 93:5).

In this verse we have the *sine qua non* of our great King: Not only is He eternally and actively in *control* of the universe which He has made, He communicates: He *speaks*. He has given testimonies. The speaking of God is a testimony of His grace and condescension. From majesty on high have come the words of His grace, the tones of His love.

Other Psalms glorify God for the manifold nature of His self-disclosure. The "statutes" or "testimonies" of this Psalm may very well be specific. That is, when the psalmist says to God in verse five that His statutes endure, he likely has in mind the specific words of God which allay all of His foes, which calm the waters and hold them in their places.

When Wisdom described her association with the God of creation, she said:

> When He prepared the heavens,
>   I was there,
> When He drew a circle on the face of the deep,

When He established the clouds above,
When He strengthened the fountains of the deep,
When He assigned to the sea its limit,
So that the waters would not transgress His command,
When He marked out the foundations of the earth,
Then I was beside Him,
   as a master craftsman;
And I was daily His delight,
Rejoicing always before Him,
Rejoicing in His inhabited world,
And my delight was with the sons of men (Prov. 8:27–31).

Here Wisdom happily boasts of God's statutes respecting the insolent waters: Their boundaries are fixed; they may not transgress His command.

Lord of Storm

We may view the words of the Lord Jesus Christ as He rebuked the wind and the raging waters of the Sea of Galilee as a part of the continuing message of Psalm 93. The incredulity of the disciples was appropriate:

> And they were afraid, and marveled, saying to one another,
> "Who can this be? For He commands even the winds and water, and they obey Him!" (Luke 8:25).

Who *indeed* is this? He is the One who *ever* calms the waters and soothes the winds, for His testimonies endure and His statutes last. He does His work with a word.

Idolatry Abounds

And since He is the one who controls the insolent waters, there is none other! Here is the rub. Our God is

King, and none other. Hence, anything else than God is a shabby substitute, vain and empty, lacking substance altogether. A presentation of the reality of the rule of God presents the specter of the false rulers proposed by mankind. These are idols.

Let us consider idolatry in a narrow sphere and in an unexpected context. An idol is any unreality, even if that unreality is perceived by one who has a veneer of faith.

I know of one man who has such an unreality in his life. It has taken on the form of a monomania, an all-consuming illness. Even though this man perceives his compulsion is a burden from the Lord, manifestly it is not. And in the process the rule of God has been denied in this man's life.

This is a man with fine training who decided that God desired him to begin a Christian school, even though the community in which he lived had existing Christian schools and presented no demonstrable need for another. Undaunted, this man sold his house and used his equity funds to purchase chalk and erasers, desks and tables, paper and staples—all the physical implements for a school. But still he had no teachers, no students, no school.

As time passed and funds were exhausted, this man left his family, a wife and four daughters, and moved to a remote wilderness area in the northwest. He now lives in a pup tent year round and writes curricula for a non-existent school. He has been there for four years now, summer and winter alike. He perceives himself to be a modern Don Quixote with an unshakable quest. He is in fact a pitiable idolater, who, worse than an infidel, has abandoned wife and children to pursue an unreality.

All about us forces are competing for the place in our lives that God demands. Whenever anything, no matter how worthy it might seem, takes the place of the rule of God in our lives, we become idolaters.

Our God Is King

Our God reigns! Any substitute for God in our lives is delusion. Psalm 93 insists that God *is* King.

His splendor is from eternity.

His stability is unchallenged.

His statutes endure forever.

The true starting point for a study of biblical prophecy is a grand and exalted view of God. Our view of the future reign of the Lord Jesus must be seen in continuity with the ongoing reign of God.

Read Psalm 93 again in your own Bible version. Though you may have looked before (even as we had looked at our "Benji"!), now do you see?

·CHAPTER 5·

An Old, Old Song

Psalm 99

The true starting point for a study of biblical prophecy is a grand and exalted view of God. One more Psalm will help us to round out our perspective concerning the new song of the coming reign of the Lord Jesus. This is Psalm 99, a poem that adds solemnity and dignity to our view of the present and future reign of Christ.

There seems, to be perfectly frank, to be so much nonsense written in the name of biblical prophecy. Could the silliness of some writings have been produced if the writers had first lingered at the waters of the music of Psalm 99? I think not. Let us linger at these waters and be refreshed by them in our perspectives of the prophetic future.

The Trisagion

If we believe that the Lord Jesus Christ is soon to come to the earth as King of Kings and Lord of Lords, we need to be impressed again with the holiness of God who *is* King over His people today. Such is the thrust of the singing of the angels in Revelation 4:8:

> Holy, holy, holy,
> Lord God Almighty,
> Who was and is and is to come.

Among my earliest memories of worshiping God is singing the hymn, "Holy, Holy, Holy!" It was the practice of our congregation to begin nearly every service by singing these words:

> Holy, Holy, Holy!
> Lord, God Almighty;
> Early in the morning
> Our song shall rise to Thee.

These splendid words of Reginald Heber and the musical setting NICAEA established the mood for our services. We had come to exalt the holy name of our God and to approve His rule in our lives.

Although I did not know it at the time, the singing of the words "holy, holy, holy" is one of the most ancient practices of the church in corporate song. In his recent book, emphasizing the life of holiness, Peter E. Gillquist writes:

> In the Lord's Prayer, Jesus taught us to pray, "Our Father [who art] in heaven, Hallowed [holy] be Your name. . . ." The angelic hosts praise the Triune God throughout eternity, singing, "Holy, holy, holy, is the LORD of hosts . . ." (Isaiah 6:3). The Trisagion (which means *thrice-holy*) Hymn, echoing this confession of the seraphim, is one of the earliest and best-known anthems of the ancient Church:
> > Holy God,
> > Holy Mighty,
> > Holy Immortal One,
> > Have mercy on us.
> Indeed, believers of all ages have everywhere ascribed holiness to the name of the Lord.[1]

Doubtless the singing of "Holy, holy, holy" throughout the history of the church goes back to the words of the

---

[1]Peter E. Gillquist, *Why We Haven't Changed the World* (Old Tappan, N.J.: Revell, 1982), p. 29. The Trisagion is also discussed by Dom Gregory Dix, *The Shape of the Liturgy* (London: Adam & Charles Black, 1945), pp. 465–70.

seraphim as heard by Isaiah in his magnificent vision of the exalted King Yahweh (see Is. 6:1–13). These were the same words John heard the cherubim singing before the throne of majesty (see Rev. 4:8).

King of Kings

Isaiah was no stranger to kings. He was related to the royal House of Judah, and he likely had access to the palace and the throne room. One day he might have been wandering through the palace as he was mourning the death of the king whose name was Uzziah (see 6:1). Isaiah may have walked into the throne room and seen the empty chair. His mind was probably filled with thoughts of the years that had passed and what might have been. He may have thought about what might be coming when a new king would soon sit on that throne.

Then all of a sudden, whether in the body or not (he likely knew not), he was transported above to the throne of glory. Never had he seen a king as this King! Of this King the angels were singing:

> Holy, Holy, Holy is Yahweh of hosts,
> the fullness of all the earth is His glory (Is. 6:3,
>   personal translation).[2]

When Isaiah says that his vision took place in the year of the death of King Uzziah, he gives us not only a chronological context, but a significant contrast as well. In the year of the death of a good king, Isaiah saw the King who is eternal, whose reign is forever, whose throne is never empty.

---

[2]See the NASB margin for a similar reading of the second colon of this verse. I have suggested that these words provide a biblical context for environmental concern: an attack upon the world which God has made is in some respects an attack upon His glory.

Woe Is Me

And how did Isaiah respond when he saw God? By small talk? By casual chatter? By saying, "How do you do?" His response was in fact one of self-abasement and abject terror:

> Then I said:
> "Woe is me, for I am undone!
> Because I am a man of unclean lips,
> And I dwell in the midst of a people of unclean lips;
> For my eyes have seen the King,
> The Lord of hosts" (Is. 6:5).[3]

In the presence of the Most Holy God, Isaiah found himself unworthy to speak and in jeopardy of his very being. By angelic intervention Isaiah was then symbolically cleansed, became interactive in the deliberations of God, and was commissioned for a life of hard service for his heavenly King.

Have you ever felt that way?

Expressible Words

Rarely in the experiences of biblical persons do we have a mystery so great as of a believer being "caught up to the third heaven" to hear "inexpressible words, which it is not lawful for a man to utter" (2 Cor. 12:2,4). The experience of David in the writing of the revelatory Psalms 2 and 110 may have been similar, as we shall see in later chapters.

While there are some words which we are not permit-

---

[3]Most translations render the verb *nidmêtî* as "I am undone" or "I am ruined." However, the root is somewhat problematic; it may also mean "to be silent." In the context of the praise of God by the angelic beings, Isaiah regards himself as unable to speak. When he thinks of his sinful state, he speaks of his lips—and the lips of his people—as being unworthy to praise the holy God.

ted either to hear or speak, the word which we are permitted both to hear and speak is the word "holy." The threefold expression of the seraphim also motivates one of the great biblical hymns for the congregation—Psalm 99.

One of the best ways to begin a study of a Psalm is to read it carefully, looking for internal indicators of structure. When we read Psalm 99 in this way we find that verse 9 is very similar to verse 5, suggesting at least a two-part development. As we read more closely, we find that verse 3 has strong similarities to verses 5 and 9. This suggests that the Psalm in fact has three movements, each ending with a declaration of the holiness of God.[4]

Psalm 99 may be read as a hymnic response to the song of the seraphim of Isaiah 6. It recaptures the mood of Isaiah and helps us to stand alongside of him in his great vision of the Lord. This Psalm is also a precursor of the Trisagion.

Great in Holiness

In the first movement of Psalm 99 (vv. 1–3) there is an emphasis on the greatness and grandeur of our Holy King. In these words we learn that *King Yahweh is great in His holiness:*

> The LORD reigns;
> Let the peoples tremble!
> He dwells between the cherubim;
> Let the earth be moved!
> The LORD is great in Zion,
> And He is high above all the peoples.
> Let them praise Your great and awesome name—
> He is holy.

---

[4]This is the conclusion of J. J. Stewart Perowne, *The Book of Psalms,* 2 vols. (Reprint ed.; Grand Rapids: Zondervan, 1976), vol. 2, pp. 205–206.

This Psalm is an example of the Royal Psalms, which speak not so much of the coming of the reign of Jesus Christ as of the present rule of God over His people Israel—and, by extension—over the church today.

Further, the *fact* of the reign of God is not emphasized in the poem so much as is the desired *response* on the part of His people to that reign. The Psalm has an antiphonal structure which enhances the responsive element. As we think in terms of the future, this poem presents attitudes respecting the coming reign of the Lord Jesus—attitudes that will mark His people.

The associations we see with God and the seraphim in Isaiah 6 and with the cherubim in Psalm 99 should be stressed. The angels—distinctive classes of angels—surround and adore His glory.

In one church where I was a guest speaker, I noted on the bulletin that just before the sermon there would be a choir of cherubs. My thoughts were mixed. How could I follow *them?* How did this church pull that off? I waited expectantly for winged angels, glorious and foreboding; I was greeted by cute little children in darling white gowns—all lace and bows—singing to adoring parents. So much for the cherubim! So much as well for awe and wonder.

Lacking Awe and Wonder

The most notable attitude lacking in many contemporary Christian communions is a sense of overwhelming *awe* at the wonder of God. He is the one who is indescribably holy; yet how carelessly we approach Him.

In small churches we often get caught up in the sameness and pettiness of our ways and feel threatened by encouragement to change or improve our worship. In larger communions we are sometimes so enmeshed in Program and Personality that God becomes an adjunct to our services instead of the center of our attention.

Popular speakers are overimpressed with their schedules and itineraries; worshipers are occupied with a thousand thoughts of their own; singers worry about notes and deacons about the collections—and somehow we leave the assembly without having been confronted by the holiness of God.

The manner in which we respond to God is the most telling and significant aspect of our life. For most of us, God is too often viewed as commonplace, not holy; as understandable, not mysterious.

Understanding God

Not long ago I found myself in an unpleasant debate with a self-taught Bible teacher who (unwittingly) had taken a heretical position in an area of major doctrinal import. This was not a discussion about the number of angels that might stand on a pinhead. This man forthrightly denied the doctrine of the Trinity. His clincher was, "Now I understand God." Stubbornly resisting the truth and insulting in manner, this self-assured man "understands" God. It is no small matter to deny the three Persons of the Trinity. But equally unsuitable is the arrogant presumption that one understands the nature of God. Listen again to the words of our poem:

> Yahweh reigns!
>   Let the people tremble.
> He is enthroned among the cherubim;
>   Let the earth shake[5]
>   (Ps. 99:1, personal translation).

In these words we stand beside Isaiah. We do not state our assurance of "understanding" God, but shake a bit in our sandals before His awesome presence.

---

[5]The Hebrew verb *nût,* "to shake," is compared by C. Gordon with Ugaritic *ntt,* "to wobble," in the expression "(the feet) wobble = one of the signs of physical collapse on getting bad news." *Ugaritic Textbook* (Rome: Pontifical Biblical Institute, 1965), 19.1641.

At Home . . . with God!

In our weakness we are prone to vacillate between being terrified of God and being thoughtless of Him. The Bible enjoins an attitude of balance. As believers we *are* to feel at home with God (see Heb. 10:19–25), but we must remember that He remains *God!*

The Old Testament writers had a wonderful term to express this tension—*the fear of Yahweh* (see Prov. 1:7). This term, when used about people of faith, was a positive expression denoting a personal relationship to God, an attitude of piety, a readiness to serve God, and a separation from evil. But the word used is still the word "fear"—a term that rules out carelessness, casualness, or conceit before God.

His Holy Name

I have some pious Jewish friends who refuse to spell fully terms for "deity" when writing. "God" is written as "G–d," and "Lord" as "L–d."[6]

We may smile at such practices, explaining them away as curious superstitions or lingering legalisms. Nevertheless, when was the last time we winced when the name of God was used lightly in a television situation comedy? Using the name of God in a blasphemous manner was once a capital offense (see Lev. 24:10–16); now it scarcely receives comment. Truly in our day God might say, "My name is blasphemed continually every day" (Is. 52:5). And this is done even by His own people.

The psalmist says that His name is "great and awesome." The words "great" and "awesome" are used together in this verse in a way that leads them to enhance

---

[6]Of course, such Jewish people refuse altogether to write (or to speak) God's name Yahweh, speaking instead of "the NAME."

each other.[7] God is great, awesomely great, in His holiness.

Psalm 99 first speaks of God's greatness among His own people, much like Psalm 76:1, "In Judah God is known;/ his name is great in Israel" (NIV). Yet what God was in Zion, He will also be among all peoples. While Psalm 99 speaks specifically of God's rule over His people Israel, God is not to be viewed as Lord of one nation only; He is universal King. Peoples and earth are to respond to Him in a proper manner (v. 1). He is not only great in Zion, but He is exalted over all the peoples (v. 2).

Just in Holiness

The second movement of Psalm 99 emphasizes the justness and rightness of the reign of our Holy God. Not only is Yahweh great in His holiness, *King Yahweh is just in His holiness.* Here is the middle section of Psalm 99:

> The King's strength also loves justice;
> You have established equity;
> You have executed justice and righteousness in Jacob.
> Exalt the LORD our God,
> And worship at His footstool;
> For He is holy (vv. 4–5).

The first movement of the Psalm stresses God's holiness in terms of His exalted Person. The second movement speaks of His holiness in terms of His excellent acts. We have here the expected balance in a declaration of praise between the concepts of *who God is* and *what He does.*

---

[7]We call this *hendiadys,* the use of two terms to express one concept. See Ronald J. Williams, *Hebrew Syntax: An Outline* (2nd ed.; Toronto: University of Toronto Press, 1976), p. 16. The AV rendering, "thy great and terrible name," sounds too negative for modern tastes; more's the pity.

Absolute Power

When we think in terms of a king, we likely find our-selves drawn to concepts of power, majesty, wealth, and pomp. But we rarely presume rectitude in a king. The old bromide of Lord Acton concerning the absolute cor-ruption of absolute power has been proven correct too many times.

Of the many kings and queens of the northern state (Israel), one evil ruler followed another. Each has the monotonous litany of evaluation: ". . . did evil in the sight of the Lord!" The southern kingdom (Judah) did have a few rulers who were "good." But their goodness was relative, episodic, and unpredictable. And these, mind you, were the kings of God's people! What must the kings of pagan nations have been like?

What a contrast is the rule of God: "The King's strength also loves justice" (Ps. 99:4).

He Loves Justice

Here is a potentate who has absolute power, but whose power is used altogether rightly. Justice with Him is not an aberration of the moment. Justice is His preoccupa-tion. It is something He loves to do.

In the first part of verse 4 the psalmist speaks *of* God. In the rest of the verse He speaks *to* God. This type of interchange animates Psalm 99, lending energy and liveliness to the poem. The writer says, "You have estab-lished uprightness,/ righteous justice in Jacob You have accomplished" (Ps. 99:4, personal translation).[8]

The Torah

When we reflect on the uprightness and righteous jus-tice that Yahweh established and accomplished in Israel,

---

[8]The original uses redundant pronouns for emphasis twice in these cola: "*You* have . . . *You* have." Here again we have hendiadys (see note 7) in the words "justice and righteousness." Hence, our rendering: "righteous justice" (an emphatic term!).

we find ourselves driven first to the Torah. It was in the Torah, the teaching mediated through Moses, that God established His excellent patterns for equity among His people. The poet of Psalm 119 may weary the modern reader, but never wearies himself in declaring the worth of the Torah. He states:

> The law of Your mouth is better to me
> Than thousands of shekels of gold and silver (Ps. 119:72).

When God's people erred from the path He had set before them in the Torah, He sent prophets to warn and reform the people and sages to reshape and restate His principles. We today are the heirs of all of these treasures, coupled to God's last words in the New Testament (see Heb. 1:1–2).

New Praise

All of these actions of God's justice and righteousness serve as a new call for praise. In the animated nature of this poem, the unknown writer gives words to the worship leaders to give commands to the community: "Exalt the LORD our God,/ And worship at His footstool" (Ps. 99:5). In response to these commands the people shout together for the second time: "He is holy"! (v. 5).

"Exalt the Lord, and prostrate yourself." These contrary motions are expressive of our rightful worship of the essence of God's holiness. With hands held high (an expression of openness), we praise His name. With knees bent and heads bowed (expressions of humility), we confess our unworthiness to be in His presence. Both these physical postures are appropriate responses to the holiness of Yahweh and should be restored to the practice of the church at large.[9]

---

[9]Gordon Borror and I discuss these issues in our book on the renewal of worship in the evangelical church: *Worship: Rediscovering the Missing Jewel* (Portland: Multnomah, 1982), Chapter 11, "The Body of the Believer in Worship," pp. 117–133.

Wholly Other

What does it mean to say that God is holy? One would like to respond with a clear answer. Unfortunately, scholars seem to be divided in their understanding of this major concept. One party of biblical scholars argues that the basic idea in the term "holy" is "purity."[10] Another group believes that the word "holy" stresses the idea of being set apart.[11]

In my own view, the second idea is the more valid. When we say that God is holy, we affirm that He is set apart, different from, unique. The concept of purity is related to holiness because God is removed from sin and impurity and is free from all limitation of character.

To affirm God's holiness is a way of speaking of His transcendence. He is above all things, distinct from that which He has made, and is not to be confused with His creation. The *otherness* of God marks Him out; it also helps us to see ourselves as we are. Hence, we should exalt the Lord and humble ourselves.

In the view of some theologians, the holiness of God is the most central and encompassing attribute of His being. William F. Kerr writes, "It is indeed the all-embracing attribute of God."[12] Our King is altogether holy. Commands to give public acknowledgment of Him and to worship Him are the most rational of all commands.

Response in Holiness

Our King is great in His holiness (vv. 1–3) and just in His holiness (vv. 4–5). In the third strophe of Psalm 99

---

[10]Thomas E. McComiskey, *qdš* in *Theological Wordbook of the Old Testament,* ed. R. Laird Harris, Gleason L. Archer, Jr., Bruce K. Waltke, 2 vols. (Chicago: Moody, 1980), vol. 2, pp. 786–789.

[11]H. P. Müller, *qdš heilig* in *Theologisches Handwörterbuch zum Alten Testament,* 2 vols., ed. by Ernst Jenni and Claus Westermann (Munich: Chr. Kaiser Verlag, 1976), vol. 2, p. 590.

[12]"The Holiness of God," in *God: What Is He Like?* ed. William F. Kerr (Wheaton: Tyndale, 1977), p. 37.

we learn that *King Yahweh responds in grace in His holiness:*

> Moses and Aaron were among His priests,
> And Samuel was among those who called upon His name;
> They called upon the LORD, and He answered them.
> He spoke to them in the cloudy pillar;
> They kept His testimonies and the ordinance that He gave
> them.
> You answered them, O LORD our God;
> You were to them God-Who-Forgives,
> Though You took vengeance on their deeds.
> Exalt the LORD our God,
> And worship at His holy hill;
> For the LORD our God is holy (Ps. 99:6–9).

The crux of these verses seems to be in the threefold response: "He answered them" (v. 6), "He spoke to them" (v. 7), and "You answered them" (v. 8).

He Is Not Silent

It is in these words that the holiness and transcendence of God find a balance in His relatedness and immanence. The God who is there is not silent.[13] From His exalted holiness—God speaks! How appropriate that the Incarnate One is called "the Word" (John 1:1). God has always been self-revealing. He actively communes with His people. The threefold statement of His speaking to His people matches the threefold statement of His holiness in this poem (vv. 3, 6, 9).

In the past the Lord spoke to His people through priests like Moses and Aaron, who represented man to God, and through prophets like Samuel, who spoke on behalf of God. All of these, priests and prophets, spoke to God. God also spoke to them; and through them, God

---

[13]Francis A. Schaeffer, *He Is There and He Is Not Silent* (Wheaton: Tyndale, 1970).

speaks still to us. He spoke in the mysterious pillar of cloud (see Ex. 33:9; Num. 12:5) and through the verity of testimony and precept (synonyms of revelation as in Ps. 19:7–9; 119:83, 95).

But finally God has spoken to us through His Son, the Lord Jesus Christ (see Heb. 1:1–2), the Priest who transcends Aaron, and the prophet who surpasses Samuel. It is only through the Lord Jesus, our Priest and our Prophet, that we may approach the Most Holy God. There simply is no other means to approach Him.

Mercy and Wrath

In His dealings with His people God is gracious and just. This is the point of verse 8: "You were to them God-Who-Forgives,/ Though You took vengeance on their deeds." Here is an exquisite balance between God's mercy and His wrath. When the New King James Version translates the first member, "You were to them God-Who-Forgives," it displays a new name for deity in the Psalms. These words speak of repentance as leading to God's forgiveness; stubbornness and rebellion call for His vengeance. It is in these words that we have a précis of God's motivation in biblical prophecy. When the Lord Jesus returns to the earth it will be to display both His grace and His wrath.

But the marvel of this Psalm—and of the God whom this Psalm blesses—is the fact that *God speaks to His people and answers their needs.*

As Samuel Davies put it:

> Great God of wonders!
> All Thy ways
> Are matchless, God-like, and divine;
> But the fair glories of Thy grace
> More God-like and unrivaled shine.

Israel's Trisagion

Psalm 99 concludes with the third command to exalt the name of God: "Exalt Yahweh our God,/And prostrate yourselves before His holy mountain./Surely Yahweh our God is holy!" (v. 99:9 personal translation).

Here again there appears to be a command used by the worship leaders: "Exalt the Lord! Humble yourselves!" These words are then followed by a congregational response, the third declaration of God's exquisite holiness in the poem.[14]

That Israel said "holy" three times should not be missed by us. It is really quite remarkable. Hebrew does not have simple forms for the positive, comparative, and superlative as we do in English. One way that a superlative is formed in Hebrew is to repeat a word. Hence, to say "most holy" in Hebrew, one might say "holy, holy."

The fact that Israel learned from the angels to say the word "holy" *three* times seems to suggest that when it comes to speaking of the holiness of God, a mere superlative will not do. The holiness of God is beyond our ability to express adequately. His exquisite holiness defies analysis.

So when Israel sang their old, old song, a *trisagion,* in Hebrew, the threefold use of the term "holy" was a most emphatic declaration. But now, in the words of Paul Harvey, we know the rest of the story. For when you and I sing our *trisagion,* with the New Testament revelation expanding our views and deepening our perceptions, we are driven to thoughts of our thrice holy God:

Holy is the Father!
Holy is the Son!
Holy is the Spirit!

---

[14]The view of a command-response litany in this Psalm was a conclusion arrived at by the writer in discussions with Dr. Robert Hubbard of Conservative Baptist Theological Seminary (October 1981). Further, I am taking the *kî* ("for") as an asseverative use ("surely!").

When we read the words of Psalm 99, we hear the angels sing, we hear Israel sing, we hear the church through the ages sing. When we read the words of Psalm 99, we hear the song of the future kingdom as well. We cannot but join in this song:

> Holy, Holy, Holy!
> Lord God Almighty!
> All Thy works shall praise Thy name
>   in earth and sky and sea;
> Holy, Holy, Holy!
> Merciful and mighty!
>   God in three Persons,
>   blessed Trinity!

Our God reigns over His people with exquisite holiness! And this is the God who shall come to reign on the earth in the person of the Lord Jesus Christ. When the song of creation is new at the return of Jesus the King (see Ps. 98), it will be a song in tune with the exquisite holiness that characterizes the person of God. Only with such a view are we prepared to think rightly about biblical prophecy.

Second Movement

Where Is Our King?

"There is also a music of the prophetic Psalms that is in a minor key and is unexpected and unpredictable, lamentive but still expectant. Examples include Psalms 10, 60, and 14."

If Song Turns Sour

It is time now for an interlude. We need to stretch our legs a bit and allow the teaching of the first section of the book to have its way with us. We began our study with an orientation to the world of biblical prophecy. This led to the assertion that many of the great prophetic themes of the Old Testament are found in the Book of Psalms and that they are expressed in the context of music. Further, the Psalms call for music in our own lives in response.

We have now looked at three of these hymns from the treasury of the Old Testament Psalter, and we have examined three major statements concerning the rule of God. First, God is the *coming King* in the person of the Lord Jesus Christ. Song will be new in all creation when He reigns (Ps. 98). Second, God *is King* as the Creator of all that exists. His present reign calls for song in praise of His majesty and stability (Ps. 93). Third, God *reigns* in exquisite holiness over His people and is to be adored and worshiped in a manner becoming to His character (Ps. 99).

These three Psalms, when taken together, suggest that sometimes our singing is monochromatic when it ought to be polychromatic. That is, we often sing only one theme, when the poems of the Bible call for a variety of colors to be used in our worship.

There are some communions who are so caught up with the concept of the return of the Lord that the ethical demands of God for this present age are neglected. There are other communions which tend to neglect the blessed hope of the return of the Lord Jesus and to think only in a remote manner of the rule of God over His people.

The Bible calls for balance in all areas of theology and practice. Our view of the return of Christ is often one of the last doctrines to be balanced with the present reality of the rule of God.

Yet, even with balance, we do not always sing. Or if we sing, we do not always do so sweetly. There are too many contrary motions in the world that often prevent our singing with triumph and expectation. How can we sing the sweet songs of the rule of God when so many evils pervade our living and sully our senses? If God is King, well, then—on with it. Where is the Christ who will come to rule?

We may be compared to the Jews in captivity who simply were not in the mood to sing the praises of God. Weeping by the rivers of Babylon at the remembrance of the glories of Zion, these singers hung harps on willows, saying: "How shall we sing the LORD's song/ in a foreign land?" (Ps. 137:4). So we hang up our guitars and unplug our synthesizers. How can we sing the sweet songs of the rule of God when we find contrary data in the details of our living? If God is King, why are there times when forces seem to overwhelm us? Why do these things seem to happen in the very moments when we are living so closely to Him?

How can we sing the sweet songs of the rule of God when we seem to be alone in the singing? Are we the only ones who know the tunes? Do not any others even care for the words?

There are times *when song turns sour.* We must learn to work through those hard times and see how they relate to our view of the rule of God in the present age and the age that is to come.

CHAPTER 6

Even So, Lord Jesus, How Long?

Psalm 10

> O Lord Jesus, how long, how long
> Ere we shout the glad song—
> Christ returneth! Hallelujah!
> Hallelujah! Amen, Hallelujah! Amen.
>
> —H. L. Turner

How long? When shall Christ return? Why does the Father delay His Son's return?

These questions have been asked throughout the history of the church. At times they have been asked in such a way as to lead to a speculative answer, the setting of a date. Such practices have done untold damage to disappointed people. In an article titled "The Danger of Mistaken Hopes," Robert G. Clouse writes: "Through the centuries, many Christians have been unable to maintain the tension of the possibility of the return of Christ in their time and have felt compelled to set the date for the Second Coming."[1] They set their dates, the dates pass, and discouragement sets in with renewed force.

At times the question "How long?" comes not from a

---

[1]Robert G. Clouse, "The Danger of Mistaken Hopes," *Handbook of Biblical Prophecy*, ed. Carl E. Armerding and W. Ward Gasque (Grand Rapids: Baker, 1977), p. 27. In this article Dr. Clouse traces the errors of date-setters through the history of the church and shows the great harm done to the cause of biblical prophecy.

misguided sense of "I want to know," but from an aggrieved conscience, a sense of moral outrage. People who feel this way want to know when the Lord will return because they cannot abide wickedness abounding, not because they want to pinpoint a date in a chart. When the question "How long?" is asked in this context, we find ourselves empathetic. We join in asking the question, "How long ere we shout the glad song?"

Since we believe that the song of worship will be new when Jesus comes, we may well ask how long must we keep singing the same old blues—or more appropriately, voicing our hymns of praise through a glass darkly—as wickedness continues to flourish and righteousness seems to be hidden from sight. Please do not misunderstand: to sing to the Lord is a glorious thing. But our ears are yet to hear heaven's hymns!

The "Why" of Outrage

This is the mood of Psalm 10.[2] And this is why Psalm 10 begins with a lamentive "Why?" The "why" of this Psalm is not one of personal hurt or pique, but of moral outrage. This is not the "Why did it happen to me?" sort of complaint, so much as it is the "Why would God allow such things to transpire on earth, if He is King?" Psalm 10 presents a time for anger.

> Why do You stand afar off, O LORD?
> Why do You hide Yourself in times of trouble?
> The wicked in his pride persecutes the poor;
> Let them be caught in the plots which they have devised
> (Ps. 10:1–2).

Why does God stand off in the distance when wicked men continually do evil deeds? If the Lord Jesus Christ

---

[2]For our present purposes, we are treating Psalm 10 as an independent unit. There are good reasons, however, which lead many scholars to believe that Psalms 9 and 10 were originally one poem. Most commentaries discuss this issue.

is going to return to the earth, why does He not do so in our own sinful age?

Think of our age and the way in which evil seems to abound at every hand. Great and little people alike are the victims. Leaders in high places seem to be regular targets of the willful acts of vicious men. Presidents are assassinated; their successors live in constant danger, likely targets for evil men against whom there seems to be only meager protection. Internationally known figures are increasingly in danger from yet another murderous attack.

Where Were You?

Who of us who were adults in the 1960s will ever forget precisely where we were when we heard the news of the assassination of President Kennedy? One did not have to be a Democrat, enthralled with America's Camelot, to have grieved deeply at that awful news—no more than one had to be black to hurt with the death of Martin Luther King, Jr., or a fan of popular music to wince with the death of John Lennon, or a Republican to be outraged again at the attack on President Reagan, or Egyptian to grieve with the death of Anwar Sadat, or Catholic to be moved at the attempted killing of Pope John Paul II or. . . .

Where *is* the Lord when world leaders are gunned down? Why is He so seemingly distant from others who are under endless attack?

I remember the day the Pope was shot. I was walking to my office and one of our professors asked me if I ever thought that in a Baptist seminary we would be praying for the survival and healing of a Pope. I told her that I would never have thought it would happen. But pray we did. All of us share in the outrage of such attacks. They are attacks against our own humanity. They are crimes against God's order.

"Why do You stand afar off, O LORD" as the wicked

attack not only world leaders, but the little, the poor, and the helpless die as well.

Do you remember that terrible, lengthy series of murders of black youngsters in Atlanta? One night we had watched the evening news and then sat down for dinner. Our son Bruce was six years old. He did not come to the table. He was in his bed weeping. I asked him what was the matter and if he was ready for dinner.

"Dinner?" he asked. "Dinner, with another little boy dead tonight?"

That series of murders may be over, but unfortunately we will not be shocked and suprised when another series begins someplace else. We will keep on hurting. And we will keep asking, as does the psalmist, "Why does God seem to hide Himself in times of trouble?" Verse two speaks of the wicked man persecuting the poor. Where is God as little people and helpless ones are the victims?

The Coyote and the Lap Dog

Recently while speaking in a church in Washington state, I stayed in a home in a remote forested area. The man of the home was sitting by a large sliding window. He had just finished his morning prayers when he looked out into his garden. There was his small dog Shasha, a Peek-a-poo, stealthily being stalked by a coyote.

The little dog was completely oblivious to her peril. In a stumbling, panicky series of motions, the man got the door unlocked just as the coyote pounced on the dog. The teeth of the coyote were deep in the shoulders of his prone prey, but the commotion at the window had caused the little dog to turn slightly, saving its life. Angry, the man yelled, threw rocks, and chased the coyote for some distance. Then he tenderly carried his little dog inside. Although the little dog was injured and frightened, it survived.

All of this we understand. What we do *not* understand is why God does not act in roughly the same way, without the stumbling. Where is the fire from heaven, the plagues, the angels? Where is God when the wicked stalk after helpless and defenseless people as a coyote after a lap dog? Why does He not storm through His cosmic "patio door" and roar and rescue? Why is the coming of the Lord Jesus delayed while His people are suffering by day and languishing by night?

Helplessly and hopelessly we watch and wait for the fulfillment of the promise of our Psalm: "Let [the wicked] be caught in the plots which they have devised."[3] But these old words seem only a vent for our distress, not a solution for our difficulty. And so we wait. We wait and we wonder.

Attitudes

In the words of the first movement of Psalm 10 we find ourselves *in distress, and we long for God's intervention.* In the second movement of the Psalm, there is a description of the wicked. We find that *in haughtiness, the wicked assume that there is no requital.* These are the awesome words:

> For the wicked boasts of his inner cravings;
>   He blesses the greedy
>   and he condemns Yahweh.
> As for the wicked, in the haughtiness of his scorn:
>   "There is no requiting;
> There is no God!"
> Such is the sum of his thoughts
>   (Ps. 10:3–4, personal translation).[4]

---

[3]The NIV reads this colon differently, as a result of the wicked acting upon the weak: "who are caught in the schemes he devises." The line is difficult, but my rendering is similar to that in the NASB and the NKJV.

[4]The Hebrew text of verses 3–4 has been subject to a variety of renderings. In verse 3 my rendering is closer to the NIV than the NASB; the latter has a similar reading in the margin. In verse 4 we have an exceedingly difficult line, but I believe that the accents and meter allow best the reading that I have given. The key term of the Psalm is

While the first section of the Psalm deals with attitudes of the *righteous,* the second section addresses the attitudes of the *wicked.* But how is it some can be so wicked that even the world reacts against them?

The Wicked and the Wicked

We should observe that there are the wicked people, and then there are the really wicked people. Some people who do not choose to know God actually live lives that are a credit to their community. They may be involved with service organizations, neighborhood planning, and strong family life. In this type of unbeliever we often have a counterfeit of true piety. For here is a person who lives well even though he does not submit to or worship God. Such "good neighbors" are not the subject of this Psalm.

Psalm 10 describes that type of wicked person who enrages us all, believer and unbeliever. Here is depicted one of Satan's utter lackeys, out of control, whose wickedness is boundless, whose conscience is seared, whose humanity is beastly.

Parodies of Praise

The psalmist describes such ones as parodies of piety. These are those who turn praise inside out.

The most characteristic word for praise in the Old Testament Psalms is the Hebrew word *hālal,* "to be excitedly boastful." A synonym for this word is *bārak,* "to

---

the verb "to requite, to seek," with God as the subject (see verses 13 and 15). In my translation *bal-yidrôsh* does not describe the man ("he does not seek *Him*"), but the man's view of God ("*He* does not seek him"). That is, he believes that God, if there is a God, simply does not care. Verse 13 explains this more fully: "He has said to himself, 'You will not seek / requite it.'" Verse 15 climaxes with the words, "Seek / requite his wickedness until You find none."

bless."[5] These words of praise are designed to be used to boast in God, to adore His name.

But the wicked take the terms of faith and use them faithlessly. Instead of boasting in God (as in Psalm 113), they boast in their own wicked intents, the dark cravings of their fallen souls. Instead of marking out God as the source of their blessing (as in Psalm 103:1–2), they bless instead those most like themselves—the greedy, the rapacious. And what is their thought of God? Absolute contempt! They hate Him. If they think of Him at all, it is with darkened disdain.

As I think about the psalmist's words in their prophetic implications, an idea presents itself concerning these wicked men. Many times in the Psalms the description of the righteous man seems to go beyond applications to mere men, whether the apparent subject is King David or another. We find in these words thoughts that find their fulfillment only in the Person and work of our Lord Jesus Christ, God incarnate. The ideally righteous Man in the Psalms is ultimately Christ.[6]

May there not be a corresponding greater reality in the descriptions of the wicked in such poems as Psalm 10? Do we not have here not only a description of evil as it is found in many men, but of evil as it will be revealed in the man of sin, the Antichrist who is the embodiment of antipiety?

The Beast

If this line of thinking is correct, then the incidents of evil that mar our living today are pale shadows of the

---

[5]I have developed the principal words for the vocabulary of praise in *Praise! A Matter of Life and Breath* (Nashville: Nelson, 1980), pp. 64–69.

[6]Bruce K. Waltke, "A Canonical Process Approach to the Psalms," in John S. Feinberg and Paul D. Feinberg, *Tradition and Testament: Essays in Honor of Charles Lee Feinberg* (Chicago: Moody, 1981), pp. 3–18.

wholesale acts of desperate wickedness that are coming in the wicked one who will function in the period before the return of Christ to the earth.

When John speaks of the man of sin, he calls him Antichrist (see 1 John 2:18). As Christ is perfect Man, the Antichrist is antiman. Is that not why the word "beast" is so appropriate for him? (see Rev. 11:7, et seq.) For one can only be truly human as one relates to God. The less one knows of God, the less truly human one is. Such was the estimate of Boris Pasternak in his gripping novel of the sufferings of *Doctor Zhivago*.

As we get close to this evil man of the prophetic Scriptures, and look for what motivates him, we find the twin delusions that Satan would have all of his servants believe: "There is no requiting; There is no God" (Ps. 10:4). Here is the *Shema'* of evil, the perversion of the creed of Israel (see Deut. 6:4): "Hear O wicked ones, / there is no requital; / there is no God."[7]

This is the antithesis of wisdom which is founded on the fear of Yahweh (cf. Prov. 1:7; Ps. 111:10). These are the sum of this one's thoughts and they are the thinking of Madame Folly (see Prov. 9:13–18), a parody of Lady Wisdom (see Prov. 9:1–6).

"There is no requital," says the evil man. He believes that there is no pay off, no bottom line. Oblivious to God, uncaring about order and constraint, he acts out his evil in the most cavalier manner imaginable. Evil men today, and in the day of the psalmist, are bad enough. The incarnate evil which is to come will be so wicked the word "man" will no longer be appropriate for him: the better term is *beast*. He will be the no-man.

In Christ we have all that man is supposed to be. In the beast we have the denial of all that is Christ. Hence, we have in this beast the denial of all that is man.

---

[7]In the true *Shema'* ("Hear O Israel: Yahweh, our God; Yahweh alone!"), Israel confessed the *reality* of God and her *relationship* to Him. Life without God is a life that is not worth living. Life oblivious to God is a wasted life. Life in opposition to God is a bestial life.

> O Lord Jesus, how long, how long
> Ere we shout the glad song?

How long will wickedness abound and Christ not return? How long will the surging of the waves mirror the turmoil in man before our Lord stills the waters again?[8] How long will the activities of evil men continue unabated, and God not break in and end their power? Even more specifically, how long will *your* troubles keep on?

The third movement of Psalm 10 describes how *in disdain, the wicked act as though there were no God* (vv. 5–11). This section begins:

> His ways are always prospering;
> Your judgments are far above, out of his sight;
> As for all his enemies, he sneers at them.
> He has said in his heart,
> "I shall not be moved;
> I shall never be in adversity" (Ps. 10:5–6).

Here we sense the disdain of the wicked. Self-sufficient, arrogant, a paradigm of pride—he snorts at all foes and ignores the possibility of God. He struts his stuff with a haughtiness that seems as limitless as his own evil horizons. There is no requital, no bottom line, no pay day someday from God.

As we read the words of Psalm 10, we see how they apply to the virulently wicked in any age. As we read them prophetically we see how they portend the epitome of evil, the man of sin.

If you were a spiritual orthodontist, a dentist of the soul, verse seven describes what you would find in his mouth:

> His mouth is full of cursing and deceit and oppression;
> Under his tongue is trouble and iniquity.

---

[8]See Psalm 124:1–5; cf. Matthew 8:26–27.

These symbolic words speak of contaminating evil in an orifice that is suggestive of an active depravity which is indeed total, and in full control. When we speak of total depravity we usually mean not that every person is as bad as he might be, but that every aspect of their being is marred by sin. But here we have one in the total control of sin. Evil not only affects him, it *fills* him.

As you read these next verses of a predator stalking and killing its prey, keep in mind that the figurative language describes an attack by man on man:

> He sits in the lurking places of the villages;
> In the secret places he murders the innocent;
> His eyes are secretly fixed on the helpless.
> He lies in wait secretly, as a lion in his den;
> He lies in wait to catch the poor;
> He catches the poor when he draws him into his net.
> So he crouches, he lies low,
> That the helpless may fall by his strength (Ps. 10:8–10).[9]

Though we may sing our godly songs from the bottom of our hearts in worship and praise of God, let us not ever forget that somehow the roaring lion is yet in the listening audience!

Martyr Chester Bitterman

In this strong poetic section, which describes a predator striking his prey, I am unable to shake the association in my mind between this biblical text and the kidnapping of missionary Chester Bitterman III in Bogota, Colombia, in January of 1981. I had been studying this Psalm during those days when the news came to us that missionary Bitterman was captured by terror-

---

[9]The text of verse ten is difficult to render; translations vary considerably. However one reads the image, the conclusion is clear: another innocent victim has been destroyed by evil men.

ists. I was to find to my horror that these words of Psalm 10 take on strong associations with his death.

When Bitterman was first captured, the news was sent to Christian organizations, churches, missions, and schools all over the world. Churches prayed for him, for his wife Brenda, and for their children. Missionaries joined national believers in interceding for him. Tribal peoples and Christian scholars were united in praying that Bitterman would be delivered.

I prayed for him, and—doubtless—so did you. We prayed that his release would be accompanied by the good news that his captors themselves might have been made captive to the claims of Christ. Because of the worldwide impact of Wycliffe Bible Translators, it is possible more Christians in more places prayed for this young man in one period of time than have ever prayed for a single missionary in the history of the church.

And yet on March 8, 1981, his body was found with a fatal bullet wound, lying in an abandoned bus.

What can we say about this? Listen to what Chet said about himself in reflections written shortly before his capture: "There are times when God expects us to take a cold, hard, stubborn stand for Him. And just like Daniel and his friends in the Bible (Daniel 3), we have no guarantee of the outcome. We may have to lay our life on the line."[10]

His father, Chester Bitterman, Jr., said, "We have eight children. And they're all living: one's in heaven and seven are on earth."[11]

Perhaps the most touching are the words of his daugh-

---

[10]These words were discovered in a note on his desk calendar that was discovered months after his murder, but written before he was kidnapped. They are reported by Betty Blair, "On Life and Death: Chet Bitterman's Own Words," used by permission of *Family Life Today* (April 1982), p. 11.

[11]Chet Bitterman, Jr., "A Response of Thanks," ibid., p. 10.

ter, Anna Ruth, who at the age of four showed family friend Jack Keels a Bible story book.

"See that man?" she said, pointing to Jesus. "My Daddy's with that man. And he can talk to Him and see Him right now." She looked up into my eyes—her face absolutely radiant. "I can't see my Daddy right now, but someday I will."[12]

Chester Bitterman III joins a long, majestic line of men and women who have died in the selfless service of the Lord Jesus Christ, a line begun by Stephen, the pro-tomartyr (see Acts 7:54–60). Yet, as we read Stephen's words, we find that this line in fact began even long before him:

Which of the prophets did your fathers not persecute? And they killed those who foretold the coming of the Just One, of whom you have now become the betrayers and mur-derers (Acts 7:52).

In the words of our Lord, this line began with the blood of righteous Abel (see Matt. 23:35). And as we reflect, we conclude it centers in fact on the blood of righteous Christ (see Heb. 12:24). This is the long line of those "of whom the world was not worthy" (Heb. 11:38).

It is not a new thing for the righteous to suffer prema-ture death at the hands of evil men. It is a thing far too old. And we sigh and sing again, "O Lord Jesus, how long, how long?" And then with Psalm 10 we ask,

Why do You stand afar off, O LORD?
Why do You hide Yourself in times of trouble? (v. 1).

It would be a pleasure for me to offer a dogmatic re-sponse to this question. But as in the case of so many of

---

[12]Jack Keels as told to Betty Blair, "Seeing Daddy Again—A Child's Expectation," ibid., p. 12.

our questions to God, this is not answered directly in this Psalm or anywhere here on earth. Even so, the Psalm does not end here. Rather it surges forward to the certainty that *one day God will arise;* one day righteousness will prevail. One day Christ will return! "'Surely I am coming quickly.' Amen. Even so, come, Lord Jesus!" (Rev. 22:20).

In the interim, we suggest there are two reasons for the delay of the rising of God, of the prevailing of righteousness, of the return of Christ to the earth. These proceed from both God's grace and His wrath.

The Patience of Mercy

One reason that our Lord delays the return of Christ to the earth is explained in 2 Peter 3:9:

> The Lord is not slack concerning His promise, as some count slackness, but is longsuffering toward us, not willing that any should perish but that all should come to repentance.

The delay of Christ in establishing His kingdom on earth is a wonder of His mercy, an action of God's grace.

In whatever way we may understand the sequence of events between this movement of the Psalm and the second coming of Christ to the earth—*however* we may understand these things—we all see judgment coming. Untold anguish, unparalleled pain, indescribable terrors await those without Christ at His appearing.

The new order is not weakened at all by the gracious delay of God in bringing about the return of the Lord Jesus. It is, in fact, prompted by God's desire that the family of the faithful be made complete.

Peter follows the words of grace in verse nine with the brutal reality of coming judgment:

> But the day of the Lord will come like a thief, in which the heavens will pass away with a roar and the elements will

be destroyed with intense heat! and the earth and its works will be burned up (2 Pet. 3:10 NASB).

Peter probes us as we await the day of Christ's return. He does not call us to work out chronologies; he does not encourage us to play one-upsmanship with God in speculative thinking. There is no Bible lottery or numbers game here. Rather, the *fact* of the coming judgment is a call to us for holy living:

> Since all these things are to be destroyed in this way, what sort of people ought you to be in holy conduct and godliness, looking for and hastening the coming of the day of God, on account of which the heavens will be destroyed by burning, and the elements will melt with intense heat! But according to His promise we are looking for new heavens and a new earth, in which righteousness dwells (2 Pet. 3:11–13 NASB).

As we look forward to a kingdom of righteousness—in which kingdom the righteous One Himself will dwell with us personally and visibly—we are called to live lives of righteousness ourselves, in conscious expectation, remembering that God's delay is for the salvation of others who have not yet experienced His saving grace (2 Pet. 3:18).

The Patience of Wrath

A second reason for the delay of God's answer to our lamentive cry, "How long?", is bound up in His wrath. Not only does God's patience allow time for the salvation of the full complement of God's people, it also allows for the full effulgence of evil among those who continue to reject Him.

When God established His covenant with Abram at the dawn of Israel's experience, He did so in an incomparable act of condescension to the culture of that day. If we extrapolate from the picture given in Genesis 15:8–17, it appears that solemn and binding treaties might have been made between men in those days by their taking a number of animals, killing them, cutting them in two, and then aligning the parts to form two grisly lines. We may presume that each of the contracting parties would then have walked between the parts, as an unforgettable symbolic act: "If I do not maintain my part in this treaty, may I become as one of these!"

In this case Abram took three animals (a heifer, a goat doe, and a ram) and two birds (a dove and a pigeon). He killed them all, cut the animals in two, and lined up the parts in two lines. All day long he guarded this awful pathway by driving away birds of prey, perhaps even flies, from the carcasses.

Then came darkness. Abram was put into a deep trance. An unnatural heavy darkness, a terror-laden blackness came upon him. And God was there!

Abram did not walk between the parts. He could not. In his trance, in the deep darkness, a smoking and flaming symbol of God's presence mysteriously went between the parts of these slain animals. This was a covenant whose ultimate fulfillment depended on God. *God* placed Himself under the onus and obligations in this unforgettable drama!

Not only was God there, He also spoke. And the words He spoke related both to Abram's future (see v. 15) as well as to an outline of the history of Abram's descendants for the next four hundred years (see v. 13). He told Abram of the descent of Israel to Egypt, of their long servitude there, of their eventual deliverance by the hand of God, and of their triumphal conquest of the land of Canaan.

In the context of this covenant, God said to Abram of the peoples of Canaan, "the iniquity of the Amorite is not yet complete" (Gen. 15:16). This is almost a parody of the overflowing cup of blessing in Psalm 23:5. There is a cup of iniquity, and it is being filled. When it is overflowing, then God will bring judgment.

With this perspective, I believe we have a new understanding of the ban (Hebrew *ḥerem*) that God placed on Jericho (see Josh. 6:17) and the dispossession of the inhabitants of Canaan which was ordered by God (see Josh. 3:10, cf. Gen. 15:18–21).

The conquest of Canaan may be seen as *a paradigm of final judgment*. To the extent that Joshua failed to accomplish the task, either by sham alliances (as with Gibeon [see Josh. 9]) or by incomplete victories (as suggested by Joshua 13:1–6), the analogy fails; for in final judgment there will be no weasel deals and none slipping through the net.

But God is delaying the establishment of the kingdom of the Lord Jesus on earth today for the same reason He delayed Israel's conquest by Abraham's descendants—that the iniquity of wicked men and women be complete and none be able to charge Him with injustice when the final judgment comes.

So let us not ask incessantly, "How long, Lord Jesus, how long?" For when the end comes, there will be the completion of God's grace and the full preparation of God's wrath.

The Victorious Prayer

But one day God will arise!

> My Lord, what a morning,
>   when the stars begin to fall!

Listen again to the words of Psalm 10. This is the fourth movement, where *in confidence, we pray for God's intervention.*

> Arise, O LORD!
> O God, lift up Your hand!

Do not forget the humble.
Why do the wicked renounce God?
He has said in his heart, "You will not require
an account."
But You have seen it,
for You observe trouble and grief,
To repay it by Your hand.
The helpless commits himself to You;
You are the helper of the fatherless.
Break the arm of the wicked
and the evil man;
Seek out his wickedness until You find none
(Ps. 10:12–15).

In these strong words of renewed confidence, we pray
for God's will to be done on earth as it is done in heaven,
that His kingdom truly come—much as Jesus did in the
Lord's Prayer.

The words "Arise, O LORD" in Psalm 10:12 reflect the
similar words of the sister Psalm 9,

Arise, O LORD,
Do not let man prevail;
Let the nations be judged in Your sight.
Put them in fear, O LORD,
That the nations may know themselves to be but men
(Ps. 9:19–20).

You see, one day Yahweh will rise from His heavenly
throne. There will be no stumbling, no frantic moves or
wasted effort. When God arises, it will be with purposed
terrors, with predetermined judgment.

The wicked, who have energized their lives in the belief that God "will not require an account" (v. 13), find
that there is in fact a payoff, a bottom line. God is oblivious neither to the grief of the righteous nor to the depravity of the wicked.

Are we outraged when evil men pounce on the innocent like a coyote on a lap dog, and is not our Father

aggrieved? Do we deplore attacks on world leaders, and is not God enraged? Do we hurt when children are abused, the righteous are defrauded, and evil abounds— and does not the Lord of glory take it to mind? Do we teach uprightness? Do we urge equity upon Him?

Is He not about to burst into our age, to bring about His *own* great will, according to His promise, that kingdom "in which righteousness dwells" (2 Pet. 3:13)?

We *do* pray, "Thy Kingdom come." We do pray for an end to wickedness. For the end of evil must come. But when we pray this prayer, it is never casual.

The King Is Coming

Now comes the new perspective at the close of Psalm 10. In the fifth and final movement, *in faith, we assert the triumphal reign of our great King.*

> The LORD is King forever and ever;
> The nations have perished out of His land.
> LORD, You have heard the desire of the humble;
> You will prepare their heart;
> You will cause Your ear to hear,
> To do justice to the fatherless and the oppressed,
> That the man of the earth may oppress no more
> (Ps. 10:16–18).

In these verses we are taken by prophetic perspective to the time of the eternal reign of the Lord Jesus the King. The kingdom of God is seen to be realized on earth in the prophetic stance of this strophe. These words present the fulfillment of God's promise, and they come in response to the prayers of countless believers from the time of the Old Testament temple to the period of the church today.

The great King Jesus is recognized and owned as the eternal Monarch of heaven and earth in these verses. His reign is proclaimed to be without end.

To accomplish His rule and to realize His reign, a great battle needs first to take place. This battle is alluded to in this Psalm in the words describing the passing away of the nations from the land. The details of the battle of the end times are given in another Psalm, Psalm 110, which we will study in a coming chapter.

Entire nations have now perished. The wicked are no more. In the future stance of these closing words of the poem we learn that evil men of earth shall never again terrify the righteous. To the defenseless, God is Defender. For the helpless, Christ is Helper. For the fatherless, God is Father. For the widow, He is Husband. For the needy, He is Succor.

Enough Is Enough!

And He will do it all in keeping with His character. "O Lord Jesus, how long?" Well, *long enough that the delay of God in sending His King will have displayed His righteousness and His mercy.*

The principal reason the Scriptures warn against date-setters[13] is that they do not take into account the reasons for God's delay in sending Christ to earth as glorious King. His righteousness will be seen in the full complement of the people of God. His righteousness will also be seen in the awful display of His wrath.

How long? By His grace, long enough for the wicked to come to repentance and long enough for you and me to practice holiness in an evil day—and to do so with a song of praise to the King who reigns and who *is* coming again in glory!

---

[13]See again Matthew 24:36: "But of that day and hour no one knows, no, not even the angels of heaven, but My Father only."

· CHAPTER 7 ·

A Song of Struggle

Psalm 60

God moves in a mysterious way
His wonders to perform.

—William Cowper

We believe the King who is coming is King even now. And yet many things may cause our song of praise to the rule of the King and our anticipation of the return of Christ to turn sour. In our study of Psalm 10 we found that a sour song may come from a sense of social injustice and moral outrage. Where is the King when wickedness seems to be unrestrained? Where is the return of Christ when evil abounds?

Another pressure that may cause us to have a sour song of praise to God comes when we feel that forces are conspiring against us in an *unfair* manner, often at the very time we are attempting to live for the Lord. Perhaps you have just made a new kind of commitment to Christ, a fresh vow of trust, and then something goes amiss—a loved one dies, you are demoted or maybe fired, there is a split in your church. What happens to our doctrine of the rule of God when it seems that even He has turned against us? If God is not for us, who needs the return of Christ?

Psalm 60 begins in this way:

You have rejected us, O God, and burst forth upon us;
    you have been angry—now restore us! (Ps. 60:1 NIV).

In this statement of complaint, the community is being led in a lament against God who, it seems, has burst out upon His people without cause, without reason. Such a feeling does little to encourage us to sing the praise of God as King today, much less of God as King tomorrow.

The Paycock

Juno and the Paycock is a work by the Irish playwright Sean O'Casey. Set in the troubled Twenties, this somber play chronicles the disintegration of an Irish family (a microcosm of the nation). The Paycock is a wastrel who always has plans for a brighter tomorrow. In the village pub, with a glass of beer in hand, he struts about and tells all who will listen how things will be better—very, very soon.

Juno, his wife, is the only stable one in the family. But at the end of the play, even Juno has left the Paycock. Their daughter has had a disastrous affair with an Englishman. She is now pregnant and alone, and the family is disgraced by her. She wanders off to an uncertain fate. The son is assassinated by a rogue crew of IRA insurgents because of an earlier act of treachery on his part.

Undaunted, the Paycock fills his home with rugs and furniture, on the promise of a legacy that never materializes. Then the movers come and strip his rooms bare of all finery.

At the end of the play, the Paycock has lost his family: his wife is gone, his daughter is in disgrace, and his son is dead. Only his old drinking buddy is with him, but even Jocko is about to leave.

He'll not strut again, this Paycock. He is lying on the bare floor. With a fist slamming on the floorboards, he screams, "Life is in a terrible state of chassis!" As Jocko looks on, an unsympathetic observer to the ruined "chassis" of the Paycock's life, the lights go out and the curtain falls.

Disheartening, isn't it? Especially when you are the Paycock, aware that your life and world are in "a terrible state of chassis." King David knew the same sorrow. In the words of Psalm 60, he screams as strongly as the Paycock did. David's lament includes both strong emotion and dark charges. His world was in a terrible state. But that which intensified his despair was the fact that he had trusted in God, he had believed in the King, and he had expected things to get better. But they didn't. God, it seemed, had let him down. He writes,

> O God, You have cast us off;
>   You have broken us down;
> You have been displeased;
>   Oh, restore us again! (Ps. 60:1).

Trick, But No Treat

There is no new song in the life of the Paycock. But then we did not expect one, for he was not portrayed as a man of faith in God. What hurts us more deeply is to witness a man or a woman of faith who thinks that God has abandoned them.

We have a friend, a lovely young woman, who loves God and truly wishes to order her life to His glory. One day I asked her how she was. As she answered honestly, my heart broke along with hers.

She had been going with a young man for some time, but had resisted his suit in marriage as she was not sure he was a believer. Somehow, she suspected that his interest in church was demonstrated only to please her.

But one day she decided that he was a believer, that she would marry him, that he was the right one for her. After work she went to his home on that Halloween to meet him for a dinner date. She planned to accept his proposal for marriage that night.

When she knocked on the door, he did not respond at first. But then he told her to come in, that the door was not locked. Puzzled, she entered the home but found that he was not in the living room. Then she heard his voice again: "I'm in here." She followed the voice to his room and found him in bed with another woman, a friend of hers. This was his cute way of saying that he wanted no more of her and her Christ.

She found herself running down the street. Her throat was sore; she realized she had been screaming. As she concluded this story, she looked at me and asked, "How can people who say they love me do things like this to me?" Then she added, "How can God let something like this happen?"

My friend's question is far more wrenching to me than the scream of the Paycock. She had trusted God and had expected better from Him. Later on she would see that God had spared her, but at the time she felt God had let her down. The Paycock trusted only in himself and had himself alone to blame. When one's throat is sore from screaming that God has rejected him—that is a sore throat that needs a great deal more than a lozenge. In addition to a topical treatment, there needs to be a new experience of the reality of God. So it is in Psalm 60.

The First Movement

Here is the first movement of Psalm 60. As you read these words, see if you can sense how sore David's throat might have been in his helpless scream to God for deliverance.

> O God, You have cast us off;
> You have broken us down;
> You have been displeased;
> Oh, restore us again!
> You have made the earth tremble;
> You have broken it;
> Heal its breaches, for it is shaking.
> You have shown Your people hard things;

You have made us drink the wine of confusion.
You have given a banner to those who fear You,
That it may be displayed because of the truth.   Selah.
That Your beloved may be delivered,
Save with Your right hand,
   and hear me (Ps. 60:1–5).

In this first movement of Psalm 60 we read that *from their helplessness, God's people scream out to Him for deliverance.* The intensity of the scream to God is suggested by the type of verbs used and the number of accusations brought against Him. Listen again to the level of lament against God:

> You have cast us off.
> You have broken us down.
> You have been displeased with us.
> You have made the earth tremble.
> You have broken it.
> You have shown Your people hard things.
> You have made us drink the wine of confusion.

This is an extraordinary litany of lamentation; God is charged with bringing great and undeserved evil upon His people.

Patterns of Lament

Psalms of lament exhibit certain patterns.[1] Often three pronouns will be used in the lament proper. The psalmist will speak of himself (or of the community) by saying "*I* am hurting" (or "*We* are hurting"). He may then say of God, "*You* do not care." And then he may refer to his enemies by saying, "*They* are prevailing." In this pattern the theology of the psalmist ("God is good")

---

[1]I have developed the pattern of the Psalms of lament in my book *Praise! A Matter of Life and Breath* (Nashville: Nelson, 1980), pp. 34–39, 150–165, 181–197.

is tested by his experience ("life is tough"), leading him to state strong feelings of helplessness and hopelessness.

In Psalm 60 there is disproportionate attention given to the "You" element; God is charged with uncharacteristic acts which have left the people stunned, hurt, angry, staggering as though from bad wine. The point seems to be that such actions by God are not only unexpected, they are undeserved.

As in the case of my friend who was hurt so badly by the young man she thought she loved, the thing that hurt the most was that it seemed so undeserved. Sometimes we feel the chastening hand of the Lord. While that is never pleasant, at least we know that it is fair, it proceeds from love, and it is for our good (see Prov. 3:11–12; Heb. 12:5–11).

But when one is sincerely living for the Lord and then feels the heaviness of His hand, it seems so unfair! I know of a young family who live in an area of northern California that suffered terribly from torrential rains, flooding, and mudslides. Their own home was completely destroyed. The massive wall of mud that once was a hill behind their house crushed and scattered their home over a large area.

Friends of the family went on the Saturday following the storm to see if they could salvage anything of the mementos of a lifetime. They found only a few shattered belongings, all useless items. One man dug down through some six feet of mud and debris. He found a small section of a bookcase and three partially damaged books. When he examined the titles he found them to be almost eerie. The first was the *Reader's Digest Complete Book of Home Repairs*. The second was the Morris and Whitcomb book, *The Genesis Flood*. The third was the prize—Francis Schaeffer's title, *How Should We Then Live?*

Could it be that God was having a joke at their expense? Those three titles in that context seemed nearly too ironic to endure.

Undeserved Actions

Can it be that God *ever* has a joke at our expense? Did not David wonder about that same thing as he wrote these words of excruciating pain?

From the hints in the superscription to this poem, I believe that we can partially reconstruct the circumstances that led to David's lament. We know from 2 Samuel 8 that David expanded his kingdom with God's direction and blessing by achieving victories over all of his foes. The account given in this chapter is of one victory after another.

What we are not told in 2 Samuel 8, but are told by the contents of this Psalm, is that on one of David's great campaigns of conquest he suffered a terrible defeat that was unexpected and undeserved. In David's campaign against Edom (mentioned briefly in 2 Sam. 8:13–14; 1 Chr. 18:12–13), they were attacked by surprise by armies from Aram-naharaim and Aram-zobah.

But in this defeat, David was not receiving punishment that he deserved. This is not a penitential Psalm (as Psalm 51). David was doing the work of the Lord when he was stricken. He could not understand it. Hence, he cried out to God from utter helplessness.[2]

As is fairly well known, wine in the Old Testament is spoken of in a figurative sense both in terms of blessing (see Ps. 104:15) and cursing (see Is. 51:17). When David wrote that God had caused him and his people to drink "the wine of confusion" (Ps. 60:3), he was referring to wine in the judgmental sense. Later Jeremiah developed this image in a vivid description of deserved judgment on Judah and the nations:

---

[2]In the reconstruction of events I am giving I am taking very seriously the Davidic authorship indicated in the superscription, a view not held by many commentators today. A discussion of other views is given by J. J. Stewart Perowne, *The Book of Psalms,* 2 vols. (reprint ed.; Grand Rapids: Zondervan, 1966), vol. 1, pp. 468–70.

For thus says the LORD God of Israel to me: "Take this wine cup of fury from My hand, and cause all the nations, to whom I send you, to drink it. And they will drink and stagger and go mad because of the sword that I will send among them" (Jer. 25:15–16).

Jeremiah then describes how he took the loathsome cup and gave it to the many nations that the Lord commanded to drink from it (vv. 17–26). He was then given these charming words of "toasting," these bitter "cheers."

"Therefore you shall say to them, 'Thus says the LORD of hosts, the God of Israel: "Drink, be drunk, and vomit! Fall and rise no more, because of the sword which I will send among you"'" (Jer. 25:27).

Such is the latent meaning in the expression of David's lament. He and his men were given a defeat which was like the terrible judgments of God, a defeat that might be likened to a cup of bad wine. Then would come the reeling, the physical illness, and death—and it was all so unfair!

Expected Actions

In verses four and five of Psalm 60, David turns from lament proper to confession of trust and petition for deliverance. These verses are notoriously difficult to translate. You may compare any two translations of the Psalms to see how varied they are. Here, in my personal judgment, is the best solution of these hard, but majestic lines:

You have given to those who fear You
    a banner   Selah
  for rallying from before the bow,
In order that Your beloved ones might be delivered—

Save us by Your right hand—O answer us! (Ps. 60:4–5
personal translation).[3]

Because of the structure of the lament Psalms, we expect a statement of confidence to follow even the most strident of laments. If my interpretation is correct, David is reasserting his theology of faith: God acts in ways that are fitting to His perfect character. In the most difficult of times, whatever the nature of the difficulty, God provides a way of escape.

When the people of Israel suffered from the bites of "fiery serpents" in the wilderness, they were undergoing a deserved judgment (see Num. 21:4–9). But even in that time of terrible judgment, God provided a way of escape. Moses was instructed to make an image of the serpents and set it on a pole for people to see. If anyone who had been bitten looked at that serpent, he would live.

So David pleads to God to act on our behalf *in character*. It is time for another banner to be held up high that we all might escape the bowmen that so hotly pursue us. David embellishes his words of confidence and petition by reminding God of the nature of the ones making the prayer. He speaks of himself and his people as those who fear the Lord (v. 4) and as His beloved ones (v. 5).

Then the appeal is made for the Lord to stretch out that right hand of deliverance. What an old song that is!

---

[3]Compare the NASB: "Thou hast given a banner to those who fear Thee, / That it may be displayed because of the truth. [Selah.] / That Thy beloved may be delivered, / Save with Thy right hand, and answer us!" The NIV reads: "But for those who fear you, you have raised a banner / to be unfurled against the bow. [Selah] / Save us and help us with your right hand, that those you love may be delivered." Commentaries differ greatly on these verses.

The term "Selah" seems to be placed in a strange position in this section, for it does not come at the end of the strophe nor at the major point. It is used, in fact, as a notice of a quotation that is made. Psalm 108 is made from two Psalms. Psalm 108:1–5 is taken from Psalm 57:7–11; Psalm 108:6–13 is taken from Psalm 60:5–12.

Your right hand, O LORD,
  has become glorious in power;
Your right hand, O LORD,
  has dashed the enemy in pieces (Ex. 15:6).

The Second Movement

The second movement of this Psalm is most startling. After David's strong words of lament and his plaintive plea for deliverance, we might expect anything. But what comes next we are hardly ready for: God speaks! Right in the midst of the poem God breaks in! *From His holiness God exults in His control.* Hear the words of God:

> God speaks in His holiness,
>   Exultantly I portion out Shechem,
>   and the Valley of Succoth I measure out.
> Mine is Gilead,
>   Mine is Manasseh.
> Ephraim is My helmet,
>   Judah is My scepter.
>   Moab is My washpot,
>   Upon Edom I toss My sandal;
>   Over Philistia hangs My triumphant shout!
>   (Ps. 60:6–8 personal translation).[4]

Words of Mystery

What a mystery these words are! We might ask how they came to David, but we really cannot answer that question with certainty. The words may have come from a priest or a prophet. They may have come to David as a

---

[4]The last colon of verse 8 has its difficulties. My translation is similar to that of Mitchell Dahood in The Anchor Bible: Psalms, 3 vols. (Garden City, N.Y.: Doubleday, 1965–70), vol. 2, p. 75 ("over Philistia will be my cry of conquest"). In this way this colon speaks of the ultimate defeat of Philistia as sure.

revelation from the throne of Majesty (as in Psalm 110).

However these words came to David, they are the words of God Himself. We look in vain for a word of apology. God does not excuse His actions on the basis of a busy schedule or the many demands upon His time. God is not sheepish to the shepherd of Israel. He is exultant. He is in control. *He is King.* That is the crisp confession we must come to in our own walk as Christians.

If the Psalm were to end here, we would have sufficient material to learn the hard truth of Psalm 60 as it relates to the Kingship of God. As King, He is not beholden to His subjects to render an explanation of His dealings. We do not render such judgments, ever. *He* is King.

Words of Might

When Job was brought to the place in the extremity of his sufferings to challenge the integrity of God, he did so in words as strong as those of David. Hear Job's words from chapter 30:

> "He has cast me into the mire,
> And I have become like dust and ashes.
> I cry out to You, but You do not answer me;
> I stand up, and You regard me.
> But You have become cruel to me;
> With the strength of Your hand You oppose me.
> You lift me up to the wind and cause me to ride on it;
> You spoil my success.
> For I know that You will bring me to death,
> And to the house appointed for all living" (Job 30:19–23).

Yahweh's response to Job is much in line with His response to David in Psalm 60. He is King.

> Then the LORD answered Job out of the whirlwind, and said:

"Who is this who darkens counsel
By words without knowledge?
Now prepare yourself like a man;
I will question you, and you shall answer Me.
  Where were you when I laid the foundations of the
    earth?
  Tell Me, if you have understanding" (Job 38:1–4).

Job was never told in all his life why he suffered as he did. God's workings have a secret, hidden side. The reader of the Book of Job is let in on that secret (see Job 1–2), but the actor in the play never knows. It is sufficient for Job that God knows.

Words of Courage

You and I may suffer without the cause ever being known by us. It *is* possible that in this life we will not learn the reason why. David is not told in Psalm 60 why he suffered defeat and Job is not told by God why he suffered loss, illness, and despair. Even when the fortunes of David and Job were reversed, they did not learn why they went through these trials. We must be similarly prepared. But both David and Job were instructed by their experiences to *live courageously in an age of uncertainty.* This is our lesson as well. Even if we do not know the reason for present distress, we can take comfort in the fact that *God is King.* He is in control. And He will bring glory to Himself. May He do it through us, as prominently when things go sour as when they run smoothly!

Words of Control

Look again at the words of the central section of the Psalm. God *exults* in His control. He then gives us a geography lesson. If you have a map in the back of your

Bible you may want to look at the places mentioned in
Psalm 60:6–8.

Because David thought that God was not in control,
that He had abandoned His people and had shaken the
land, God goes to the very navel of the land of Palestine,
the city of Shechem. It was to Shechem that Abraham
first came when he entered the land of Palestine (see
Gen. 12:6). After conquering the land, Joshua brought
all the tribes to Shechem for a renewal of covenant, a
new dedication to Yahweh (see Josh. 24). Here is where
the acts of God in the land began. And it is here where
God centers His strong control. No one is going to portion out Shechem, save Yahweh alone.

Across the River Jordan, in a position analogous to
Shechem on the west side, is the Valley of Succoth. This
is the center of Trans-Jordan. God is in control there as
well. No one will set out a measuring line, save the King.

The region in which the Valley of Succoth is located is
Gilead. Similarly, Shechem is in the region of Manasseh
(which straddles the Jordan River). Not only the cities,
God says, but the regions as well belong to Him. He is in
complete control.

Then, as we think of the traditional sections of the
land of Palestine west of the Jordan, we think of
Ephraim and Judah. Both belong to God. Ephraim is the
helmet on His head. Judah is the place of His rule, His
very scepter. In these words of regal, royal designation
we renew our confidence that *God who is King is in
control.*

Words of Triumph

Verse eight presents a triptych of triumph, three pictures of the ultimate subjugation of the enemies of David:

> Moab is My washpot,
> Upon Edom I toss My sandal;

Over Philistia hangs My triumphant shout!
(personal translation).

These three pictures are wonderful in their humor
and in their force. Imagine, for a moment, God coming in
from a hard day's work. He scrubs His hands and His
overalls. Where does He toss the dirty water? On Moab!
Then He takes off His sandals. Where does He throw
them? At Edom! Then there is the picture of Philistia,
arrogant and supercilious, ever calling, "Give me a man,
that we may fight together" (1 Sam. 17:10). Unknown to
poor Philistia there is the taunt of triumph of the Living
God hanging over her that will be as sure and as deadly
as the small stone of David in his youth (see 1 Sam.
17:49–50).

Words of Comfort

In Schaeffer's words, "How Should We Then Live?"
Well, we should live with courage even in distress. We
keep trusting Jesus Christ even in our hurt. When we
really *know* God is King, then we may face the gravest
uncertainty with courage; for we know His will be the
ultimate victory. There may not be an answer to our
question, but there will be victory. Here we have the
strange but very satisfying comfort that only the redeemed can truly grasp.

This is the way William Cowper put it in his old hymn:

> God moves in a mysterious way
>   His wonders to perform;
> He plants his footsteps in the sea,
>   And rides upon the storm.
>
> Deep in unfathomable mines
>   Of never failing skill,
> He treasures up his bright designs,
>   And works his sovereign will.

Slow down now, and contemplate these words:

> Judge not the Lord by feeble sense,
>   But trust him for his grace;
> Behind a frowning Providence
>   He hides a smiling face.
>
> Blind unbelief is sure to err,
>   And scan his work in vain;
> God is his own interpreter,
>   And he will make it plain.

I doubt if a finer exposition of the theology of Psalm 60 has ever been set to music. Do you sense in these words the troubled trust that marks our poem? We err in attempting to judge the actions of God by our own feeble sense. But we triumph in the heavenlies when we keep on trusting Him. God does not play foolish jokes on His people. Rather, in mines we cannot fathom, He is treasuring up the bright designs of His sovereign will. He is King. And He is the coming One!

Words of Certainty

The words of Psalm 60:8 are not only words that have humor in them, they are also words of certainty. The traditional enemies of Israel—Moab, Edom, and Philistia—have had their days severely numbered. God's sandal of subjugation will be on the necks of all the vanquished ones. And He will do this first through David, His servant. He will do it last through Jesus, His Messiah. He can also bring about these victories through you and me, His beloved ones, as we live for Him in this age of expectation.

To review the first two movements in Psalm 60, we have seen first a scene of great distress. Verses 1–5 present David leading his people in an extraordinarily strong lament concerning a defeat that his armies had suffered by Syrian forces from the north. In that section of the poem we saw God's people, feeling abandoned, cry out to Him for deliverance.

In the second section of the poem, verses 6–8, we observed the surprising oracle of the Lord in which He attests that He is still the King and that He is still in control. In these verses God exults in His control. He does so with some humor, but the joke is never on His people.

The Third Movement

In the third strophe of Psalm 60 we listen to new words of hope; for in this section we learn that *from their hope, God's people renew their faith in Him.*

Who will bring me into the fortified city?
Who will lead me against Edom?
Is it not You, O God, who rejected us?
Is it not You, O God, who would not go with our armies?
Give to us help against the adversary,
    for vain is the salvation of man.
By God we shall do valiantly,
For He will stomp on all our foes!
(Ps. 60:9–13 personal translation).

Wistful Words

In the words of the third section of the poem there are again some very real translation difficulties. But in these words there appears to be a growing hope based on the strong intervening words of God from the preceding section. The analysis of God given by David in the first movement of the Psalm is in error. But David had stated it so strongly and felt it so deeply that he finds it hard to give it up. The words of verse 11 ask the question, Who will bring in the final victory? On the basis of the words of God in verses 6–8, the answer is clear: only God can give the victory.

Yet, David must still have struggled. Has not God forsaken us? Has He not broken out upon me? On the other hand, as an early "fiddler on the roof" thinking aloud before his God, there is no help to be found in man. Any help that he will get will have to come from God.

There it is: the very God we thought had rejected us is He who shall give us the victory! The verbal linking of verses 12 and 1 tie the Psalm together. The very One that was believed to have been the source of our disaster can be the only means of our salvation. These words point us to the future.

Prophetic Words

The words of the third movement of the Psalm embolden David and his officer corps to action. They lead the men in a new attack on their foe. And they win. God gives them the victory!

The superscription of our Psalm concludes with these words: "and Joab returned and killed twelve thousand Edomites in the Valley of Salt." Once the Psalm was written and given over to the community for public singing and worship, this notice helped the people to remember the ultimate victory that lay beyond the words of the poem itself.

The Psalm was written to speak of the mood of David and the people following the initial defeat by the armies of the Syrian marauders. Given a new spirit by the Word of God which attested His control, the armies of Israel were able to defeat their principal enemy and vindicate the rule of the King. And thus these words of the third movement speak far into the future. For they portend the eventual victory of the greater son of David, the Lord Jesus Christ, against all foes at every hand. We shall see more of this in our study of Psalms 2 and 110 later in this study.

Discord and Concord

One of the great values of having a young person in
the home who is studying music is that the entire family
gets to learn the music along with the one who is playing
it! During one period, our son Craig was working on one
of the Chopin preludes. It was Number 15 in D-flat Major, sometimes called "Raindrop." I began to reflect on
that wonderful composition as I heard it played over and
over one night.

I decided the element I loved the most about that pre-
lude is the section where the right hand plays a series of
very close harmonies of alternating discord and concord.
The exposed notes in the high treble clef are called
"second intervals." That is, they are two notes with an
interval of only a one-half step or a full step. But in
"Raindrop" these potentially grating sounds are carefully resolved. This tension and release pattern greatly
heightens the effect of that work.

In thinking about these chord patterns, I wondered
what it might be like if those close discords were to be
played incessantly without ever resolving them. If such
chords were played often enough and loud enough, one
would surely develop a headache. If the discordant notes
continued over an extended period of time, some would
get physically ill. If the sounds were never to let up at
all, some would lose their sanity. Remember—these are
chords used by Chopin to portray great beauty. But the
beauty is only to be heard as the discords resolve into
pleasing harmonies.

Can we not think of the times of distress in our lives as
discords in transition? In times of great distress, the
Composer of the universe is allowing those astringencies
to occur that He may then bring about the resolution.
All of this, we believe, will lead to the great music of
praise to His name. It would seem that this very concept
of composition lies behind Psalm 60. The movement

from the discord of despair to the resolve of renewed praise is what leads to the great beauty and integrity of the poem.

Our Words

The words of Psalm 60:11–13 come down to us over the centuries with great meaning. They are as fresh today as ever they were. God is King, and the King is coming. Although His ways are mysterious, they are indeed His ways. And He will bring glory to Himself through them. For this reason, the words of this old Psalm become our words as we may face a crisis of doubt concerning the care of God and His steadfastness. It is as though this Psalm were written especially for us in the twentieth century when we go through such experiences. Let me give an example.

On the day after Thanksgiving, 1978, I was sitting beside a small pond in the courtyard of the Indonesian embassy in the city of Singapore. The total events of the day are much too involved to relate here. But you do need to know I was sick to my stomach as I sat beside the pond; I had come to the conclusion through the events of the day that God had rejected me. It all boiled down to one central problem: I had been unable to acquire a necessary visa to enter Indonesia, and thus I could not purchase the last leg of my airline ticket for my flight to Kalimantan (Borneo).

The agent for the airline had moved back to Jakarta. He had not sold his franchise to another in Singapore. Without the ticket I could not get the visa. It was Catch 22.

Then I remembered the message of Psalm 60. I remembered the strong words of the Lord to David as He insisted on His control even when nothing seemed to be right. I, like David, realized anew that if I were ever to triumph, it would have to be by the intervention of the

Lord. I prayed for a new direction. That new direction took me far out of my original plans. I went all the way to Jakarta, an immense city where I had no contacts. Having to spend a night there, I remembered someone telling me that if I were ever to go to Jakarta, I might wish to spend a night at a certain missionary guest house.

I decided to go there for the night. When I arrived, I introduced myself to the resident missionary. He was incredulous when I told him my name. "You can't be," he said. "How did you get here?" Then he told me that he had been trying to reach me all over Asia to inform me that the flight I had planned to take would not work for the connections I had to make. His desire was that I would come to Jakarta from Singapore, as he had been in contact with the missionaries I was to be with in Kalimantan. He had made the necessary arrangements. But I had to get to Jakarta first. And I had had no plan to go there.

"How did you get here?" he asked again. My only response was to say that the God I had thought had abandoned me was the very One who had brought me to where He wanted me to be!

Had the King not stopped my path and blocked my flight in Singapore, I never would have arrived at my destination in Kalimantan. Beside the pond there in Singapore I grieved at God's seemingly harsh actions. In Jakarta, and later with the missionaries in Kalimantan to whom I had come to minister, I rejoiced in the exultant control that God the King displayed in my life.

Oh—back to my friend who was so filled with deep hurt from her boy friend: What is her state today? She still has tears in her eyes when she thinks about that terrible night. But then she smiles and she speaks of her closer walk with the Lord, of her new friends, and of that from which the Lord chose to spare her.

Do you see it? God is King. He *is* coming. And we

praise Him even when our songs may sound harsh and our tunes are troubled. For nothing in our troubled times may obscure the fact that the Lord Jesus is the victorious coming King.

• CHAPTER 8 •

When Fools Sing

Psalm 14

Throughout these pages I have attempted to stress the *continuity* of the present reign of God to the future reign of Christ. God *is* King! Christ *is* returning. We who long for the coming rule are not to be ignorant of the present rule. We need to keep these twin truths in balance. This is the key to understanding the mystery and purpose of God's prophetic Word.

However, at times we may find it hard to believe in either God's present rule or in the future rule of the Lord Jesus. In fact, we face three noted obstacles as we strive to maintain our confidence in the present reign of God, and to continue our hope for the coming of Christ.

One obstacle is the *frustration* we sense concerning the delay of the King in establishing His rule and the restraint of the King in exercising His rule when moral outrages abound with impunity. The level of evil in our day seems to cry out for the King and Lord to act, for the King who is coming to come.

A second obstacle comes on a more personal level when we begin to feel that *forces beyond our control* have overpowered us, that even God is against us. In such times of genuine stress it is hard to sing the new song of praise to the rule of God now and the rule of Christ which is to come.

We have seen in Psalm 10 an antidote for the first concern of moral outrage; for the return of the Lord will be delayed long enough for both the righteous wrath and the mercy of God to be demonstrated.

In Psalm 60 we were reminded again that our God who *is* King is *King indeed* and needs no instruction from us. In the very moment in which it seems that He had abandoned us, He tends to burst in with renewed proclamation of His sovereignty and compassionate care for us. Such have been the experiences not only of ourselves, but of countless believers throughout the history of the Bible and the record of the church.

There remains a third major obstacle to a resilient faith in the rule of God in our own day. This is the increase in modern society of *indifference to God* in general and what appears to us to be the triumph of secular humanism in particular. All about us we find shrugs of complacency toward the general idea of deity, much less the personal Triune God of the Scriptures. We shall find that this modern stress is also an ancient one. It is discussed in a poetic way in the famous poem which begins, "The fool has said in his heart, 'There is no God.'" This is Psalm 14. The attitude displayed in this poem has tremendous ramifications for the future, as the age of expectancy draws to a close.

What if . . .

Have you ever wondered what it might be like if you were God? Let's suppose, for one silly moment, that this were the case. You had existed forever, from all eternity, complete in yourself, perfect and lacking in nothing.

Then, for reasons known fully only to yourself, you set about to create all that now appears out of that which does not appear (see Heb. 11:3), out of nothing. The universe you fashioned by the word of your mouth is so vast and so complex, none but yourself can really comprehend it.

Throughout the universe are vast galaxies, immense clusterings of stars that number in excess of one hundred billion. These galaxies, or families of stars, may

themselves number in the hundreds of billions—such is
the vastness of your work. Within one of these many
galaxies, each one of which you have shaped and formed
by purposeful design and intent, there is one moderate
star (of the one hundred billion that comprise a family)
about which circle nine planets. This comprises such a
minute portion of your work that only you notice this
little system.

Then comes the riddle. On one of those planets, which
the creatures who live there call Earth, there are dust-
particle beings who imagine you do not exist.

Recall that you are God in this scheme. What would be
your reaction to such impudence from such lowly
beings? Would you even notice such specks within the
vastness of your creation? And if you noticed, would you
bother even to flick away such offense, as one might dis-
pose of a bit of lint on one's sleeve, or would you let
things be for a time—and wait?

You are not God, of course—and neither am I. But
within the Book of Psalms we have access to the
thoughts of God on just such a discovery as we have
imagined. In Psalm 14 we have the singing of a fool, the
out-of-sync sounds of one who does not really know what
the song of praise is about. And in this Psalm we have
God's evaluation of such foolishness.

A Revelation of Folly

The opening verses of Psalm 14 present the concept of
the fool from divine perspective. The fool is one who
thinks it wise to deny wisdom itself. Here are the opening words of this Psalm of David, given to the director of
music for God's people to sing in contemplative worship:

> The fool has said in his heart,
> "There is no God."
> They are corrupt,

They have done abominable works,
There is none who does good.
The LORD looks down from heaven
   upon the children of men,
To see if there are any who
   understand, who seek God.
They have all turned aside,
They have together become corrupt;
There is none who does good,
No, not one (Ps. 14:1–3).

One of the amazing departures from biblical thought
in ours or any age is that a person is often thought to be
wise, not on the basis of what he affirms but on the basis
of what he denies! The first concept to be denied by the
falsely wise is the very notion of deity.

We are aware that a major modern state is based on
the philosophical premise that there is no God. In the
Soviet Union there are occasional attempts to pretend
that the government allows the free expression of religion. But those attempts to placate Jews and Christians
in the West are countered by repressive acts that are
numerous and severe.

An official reprimand came to a leading Soviet writer
who dared to suggest even in a cautious way that there
might be a God. Vladimir A. Soloukhin, a famous poet
and essayist and a Communist party member for thirty
years, recently wrote in a major Soviet literary journal:
"In the twentieth century, there is no doubt for every
reasonable person that a supreme reason exists in the
world, in the universe, in life." Soloukhin now faces re-
pression for these rather bland words, for "flirting with
God."[1] In some places one may not openly speak even of

---

[1]This story is reported in the *E.P. News Service* (24 April 1982), p. 6,
under the heading: "Soviet Party Member Accused of 'Flirting with
God.'" The story of the most celebrated atheist in our own country,
Madalyn Murray O'Hair, is told by her son, now a Christian, in the
book, *My Life Without God* by William J. Murray (Nashville: Nelson,
1982).

a "supreme reason" for being, much less proclaim the God of reality. The Gulag lives on.

Practical Atheism

It is probably not theoretical atheism so much as practical atheism that Psalm 14 concerns itself with. That is, for every individual who comes to what he or she perceives to be a rational conclusion that the proof of God lacks convincing demonstration, there are any number of people who simply could not care less if there is a God or not. Their daily living speaks of their apathy. Maclaren observed, "In effect, we say that there is no God when we shut Him up in a far-off heaven, and never think of Him as concerned in our affairs."[2] Now we are talking not of communist atheism but of capitalist atheism.

Practical atheism is that life-style in which a man wakes up in the morning after a sound night's rest, prepares for the day's work, goes about his business with strength and vigor, returns home with money earned and bills paid, shares an evening of relaxation with a lovely family—and does it without any thought of God at all.

Practical atheism is preparing meals without thinking of God as the source of food. Practical atheism is birthing babies without thinking of God as the source of life. Practical atheism is laying loved ones to rest without serious thought of God as the reality beyond the grave.

Practical atheism is using God just when it's convenient. His name helps to sanction a wedding, to formalize an oath, to intensify a feeling of displeasure, and to coat over times of unexpected grief. But the words used are hollow, empty of reality and devoid of sense. They are form but not substance. Enter nominalism.

---

[2]Alexander Maclaren, *The Psalms,* in *The Expositor's Bible,* 2 vols. (New York: Funk & Wagnalls, 1908), vol. 1, p. 125.

I am assured by a trustworthy friend that the following narrative is a true account. A few years ago a young man from a midwestern city was given an expense-paid trip to the Holy Land for a summer of study. This gift was from his home church. On his return from his summer abroad, the young man's pastor asked him to sit on the platform during the first morning service home. Then he was asked to close the service in prayer.

The pastor said, "The way you can *really* thank us is to give your prayer in Hebrew." In Hebrew! The young man had learned a few words while he was in Israel, but he had certainly not learned enough of the language to phrase a prayer. What should he do? If he owned up to his inability, would they ask for their money back? And what of the embarrassment to his parents? So he decided to wing it.

This was his prayer. He began with *abenu bashamayim*. This was a fine start: "Our Father who is in heaven." Then there was a pause, a long pause. Then he said these words, slowly and with much feeling: "*eḥad, shenayim, shelōshāh, arbā ʿāh, ḥamîshāh, shishāh, shibʿāh, shemōnāh, tishʿāh, asārāh. Amen.*"[3]

Amid the clutter of approval from the congregation must have been the parental words, "That's our boy." But actually what the rascal had done was count in Hebrew from one to ten!

A smiling Providence allowed a Hebrew-Christian couple to be in that church that morning. At the door, as people gave our young man their greetings, the Hebrew-Christian gentleman leaned up close and whispered, "Had you been there ten more weeks, 'eleven, twelve, thirteen. . . .'"

It is quite possible for one to make the right-sounding noises—and to fool even the people of God—and yet to

---

[3]For those who might observe such things, I have not attempted to show the doubling of some letters in these words.

say words that are hollow, devoid of meaning and reality. So it is with so many. We may use the word "God" as a convention of language, but not in spirit and in truth. The name of God is just a cipher. Lord, have mercy and deliver us from such deceit.

Such a one, Psalm 14 terms "fool." The term in the original text is given without the article. It is not a particular fool that is in view, but that general class of humanity who behave in foolish ways.

The Hebrew term for "fool" in this chapter of the Bible is not one that speaks of intellectual deficiency. Rather, the picture of the fool in this Psalm is one of religious and moral insensitivity. The fool is not lacking in intelligence, he is rather lacking in wisdom. He is impious, presumptuous, and churlish.

It is the same type of individual as described in Isaiah.

> The foolish person will no longer
>   be called generous,
> Nor the miser said to be bountiful;
> For the foolish person will speak
>   foolishness,
> And his heart will work iniquity:
> To practice ungodliness,
> To utter error against the LORD,
> To keep the hungry unsatisfied,
> And he will cause the drink of the
>   thirsty to fail (Is. 32:5–6).

Such a one is not an empty-headed ignoramus, but rather a person insensitive to the demands and dignity of the God to whom he is accountable. He is morally dense rather than intellectually inferior.

It is this type of folly that we may expect to rise more and more in our secular age. As you and I struggle to maintain our identity as Christians in an age of secular humanism, we can expect the folly of practical atheism to abound all about us. As we live in the age of expectancy for the return of the Lord Jesus, we should expect folly at times to seem to have the upper hand. During the period of the tribulation, such folly will probably surpass even the high levels of our own age. But at long last He shall come, who is the only wise God. And folly will finally be at an end!

The Folly

From the fool, then, we should expect folly. The Psalm begins with a statement of the heart attitude of the fool. It then presents that which comes from within, from the heart of a man (see Mark 7:20–23). Of the fool we read these words:

> They are corrupt,
> They have done abominable works,
> There is none who does good (Ps. 14:1).

The fool *produces* folly.

The verbs used in verse 1 are strong terms of moral perversion and corruption, of ethical and ritual abomination. Both of these verbs are joined in the same colon to intensify this grotesque parody of what man and woman were created to be in God's image (see Gen. 1:26–28; Ps. 8). The verbs are plurals, denoting the individual actions of members of the common class.

The word "corrupt" is first used in Genesis 6:11–12. It is thus reminiscent of the type of evil that ultimately brought about the great flood. The outworkings of the evil heart are practices of perversion and abomination. One does not have to go far these days to find countless illustrations of the wicked outworkings of folly by the fool: no God, no good.

The "good old days" were probably not quite as good as some remember them, but there are many elements in present society that are genuinely worse than our parents might ever have imagined a generation ago. What little we have gained in improving the rights of racial minorities, we have thrown away in our disregard for the rights of the unborn. The outworkings of the evil heart are regularly going to be practices of perversion and abomination—strong biblical language occasioned by strong actions and attitudes in our culture.

Folly is characterized in Psalm 14 as an absence of good. From the premise "no God" comes the outworking: "no good." This conclusion is general and all-embracive in verse one. Even as we read it today, we wonder if there is, in fact, *no* good in godless men.

God's Response

In Genesis 11:5 and 18:21, the stories of Babel and Sodom, we are told "God came down to see" if the wickedness of mankind was truly as pervasive and intense as a casual observation might imply.

God looked down as if through a window from heaven upon mankind. The striking word-plays that call to mind the most violent and far-reaching catastrophic judgments of the history of mankind are certainly intentional. There is likely an intentional suggestion in the common term for humanity used in this verse as well. The Hebrew expression is literally "children of Adam." In this phrase there is not only the continuity of the human race, but also a suggestion of the root of depravity and its universal extent.

God is searching out people who are living apart from Him to see if the preliminary observation given in Psalm 14:1 could possibly be correct. In terms of this poem we are led to believe that the scene is so startling that even God Himself can scarcely believe it! So God descends to test the theory of no God.

Two characteristics are sought by God in His "theoscopic" examination of mankind: (1) God desires to find men who are skillful in living; (2) God looks for those who truly search for Him. Here is a personal rendering of verse 2:

> Yahweh looks down from heaven
> upon mankind,
> To see if any act with skill,
> if any seek after God (Ps. 14:2).

The skillful life is the antithesis of the foolish life. The poem is a brief recounting of the major premise of the Book of Proverbs as Lady Wisdom presents herself to the naive as the antithesis of Harlot Folly (see Prov. 1:20–33; 4:5–9; 9:13–18). The life of wisdom is a life lived in the active recognition of God as *the* determining factor in one's existence. This is a life marked by prudence and directed toward the end of glorifying God and enjoying Him forever.

But what is the result of the examination of mankind by God Himself? In the spirit of the poem, God is disappointed. He who promised "seek and find" was not able to find, despite His great search. Thus comes God's conclusion.

> The entirety has turned,
> Altogether they are corrupted;
> There is none doing good,
> Not one solitary individual!
> (Ps. 14:3, personal translation).

Mankind as a totality has departed from God. The entire race has turned from God and remains alienated from Him in utter apostasy. The race, for all its vast potential, has become morally corrupted. We are like good milk that has turned sour.

The thesis, "There is none doing good," is repeated and then is made absolute by the emphatic, "not one solitary individual!" Paul quotes from these verses in Romans 3 and reasserts the central dictum of the Psalm: Mankind is universally corrupted and men are individually depraved. You. Me. These are Paul's words:

> What then? Are we better than they? Not at all! For we have previously charged both Jews and Greeks that they are all under sin (Rom. 3:9).

The apostle then quotes Psalm 14:1–3 as the principal Scripture that demonstrates this truth.

Even the Lord, with all of the faculties of omniscience coupled with limitless patience, earnestly peering through the windows of heaven as it were, cannot find one lone exception to the rule of moral foolishness and religious insensitivity among the sons and daughters of Adam.

A Revelation of Disaster

If the first section of Psalm 14 speaks of *the revelation of universal folly among mankind* (vv. 1–3), the second part of the poem presents a second revelation from God. These verses state *a revelation of the disaster that awaits those who continue in their folly*. Here are the verses of this strophe:

> Have all the workers of iniquity no knowledge,
> Who eat up my people as they eat bread,
> And do not call on the LORD?
> *There* they are in great fear,
> For God is with the generation of the righteous.
> You shame the counsel of the poor,
> But the LORD is his refuge (Ps. 14:4–6).

But wait a moment! As we read the above verses of Psalm 14, we find a people who were not in view in the first movement. These people are called by the Lord "My people" (v. 4), "the righteous generation" (v. 5) and "the afflicted" (v. 6).

One might well ask, *where did these people come from?*

The writers of the wisdom poems regularly speak in terms of two groups of people: the wise and the foolish, the righteous and the wicked. In order to present the strongest possible case for universal depravity, the Psalm has held off until the second movement the notion that there are in fact some people who respond to God's grace, who return to Him to become His people.

Actually the righteous in the second strophe of the Psalm came from the same place you and I have come from. We who know the Lord have come from the general family of good humanity turned bad. Before we knew Jesus Christ, we shared the common corruption of our brothers and sisters in Adam. But the gospel of God's grace has come to us. Praise Him! By His call we have responded in faith and become part of another race altogether: the family of God.

> Where is boasting then? It is excluded. By what law? Of works? No, but by the law of faith. Therefore we conclude that a man is justified by faith apart from the deeds of the law (Rom. 3:27–28).

Maclaren describes the words of Psalm 14:4: "the voice from heaven crashes in upon the 'fools' in the full career of their folly. The thunder rolls from a clear sky. God speaks. . . ."[4]

The second revelation of Psalm 14 is one of divine incredulity at the folly of the fool. In our study of Psalm 10 we expressed the human side of this dilemma; Psalm 14 presents the divine response to the same issue: How can it be that ordinary wicked men can become so *very* wicked?

---

[4]Maclaren, *Psalms,* p. 128.

In these words God is viewed as being unable to believe the enormity of the folly of those He describes as the "practitioners of iniquity." He is astonished! We should not be misled by the language of appearance and imagery: the purpose of the poet in this type of stress is not to be missed.

Three Accusations

There are three charges brought by God against the fool.

First, the fool is devoid of knowledge (v. 4a). This knowledge is the awareness of the reality of God. A fool may know a great deal, but if his wisdom is not based on reality in God, it is a temporal knowledge and is deficient before God. It is ultimately useless.

The second charge is that the wicked devour the people of God as they might eat a piece of bread (v. 4b). They consume the people of God as if it were no more unnatural than eating a meal. This conceit is enlarged upon in Micah 3:1–3.

> And I said:
> "Hear now, O heads of Jacob,
> And you rulers of the house of Israel:
> Is it not for you to know justice?
> You who hate good and love evil;
> Who strip the skin from My people,
> And the flesh from their bones;
> Who also eat the flesh of My people,
> Flay their skin from them,
> Break their bones,
> And chop them in pieces
> Like meat for the pot,
> Like flesh in the caldron."

Finally, the people who are described as the fools of this age refuse to proclaim or confess the Lord (v. 4c). For the verb in this last line of verse four is often translated "call" and is read in the sense of a failure to call out in prayer to God. But it is likely that the poet has more than prayer in mind here. The verb "to call" is often used in the sense of giving God the acknowledgement that He deserves.

Abraham, for example, built an altar in the land of Palestine at Bethel near Ai and "called on the name of the Lord" (Gen. 12:8). Those who do not *call* upon God are those who do not *know* Him and are thus deserving of His wrath (see Ps. 79:6). This verb is tantamount to an active knowledge of the Lord. Of such knowledge the fool is desperately lacking.

But there is hope for the fool as well. In Jeremiah 33:3 we read: "'Call to Me, and I will answer you, and show you great and mighty things, which you do not know.'" If a person will but pray, call out to Christ, and search for Him in prayer, faith will come. The promise of God will be secured "that if you confess with your mouth the Lord Jesus and believe in your heart that God has raised Him from the dead, you will be saved. For with the heart one believes to righteousness, and with the mouth confession is made to salvation" (Rom. 10:9–10).

One Judgment

It is difficult to emphasize sufficiently how important verse five is in the development of this Psalm, particularly as it relates to biblical prophecy. The author of the Psalm has been carried forward by the Spirit of God to the time of the final judgment of the wicked.

This verse alludes to the great white throne judgment that is also described by John in Revelation 20:11–15. In that apocalyptic judgment, the dead stand before the great King. They are judged by Him on the basis of their works and are found to be lacking in good. Since their names are not written in the Book of Life, they have no hope, no redress, no new chance. Instead, they are cast into the lake of fire (see Rev. 20:15).

Listen again to the words of Psalm 14:5.

> There they shall be in excruciating dread,
> For God is in the righteous generation
> (personal translation).

The word "there" speaks of a coming day of universal judgment. David sees the people before the King of Kings and Lord of Lords. These are the people who have denied Him, who have refused to worship Him, who have lived without Him.

The interpretation of the adverb "there" may be varied. For some it will be in the great white throne judgment. For others "there" might relate to the battle of Armageddon. But the concept is clear: terrible judgment by the King of Kings on those who chose folly rather than wisdom. Whether at the judgment throne or the final battle, there will be excruciating dread on the part of those who have rejected life and God. In that awful day, "all the tribes of the earth will mourn" (Matt. 24:30).

The Dread of the Fool

Psalm 14 describes the intensity of the terror of the fool by using two words in the original text. These may be translated "they will *dread dread*." By using the same word for both verb and accusative, David presents a picture of sudden and unparalleled horror when the fool finds out the nature of his folly and learns at the same time that there is no longer opportunity to do anything about it.

The hard fact to be recognized is that the God whom the fool had been negating was dwelling all along in the very people the fool had been devouring. This is descriptive of the suffering of God's people in all times. Yet it is particularly an apt description of the suffering of God's people during the terrible period of the tribulation. The figure of devouring God's people is intense and unpleasant, and would have particular meaning in the severe persecution of Israel and the saints in the period of the great tribulation. The fear of the fool fits the terror of wicked men in the time of the second advent of our Lord.

Folly after Folly

The almost unbelievable behavioral response of the fool is seen in verse six:

> You shame the counsel of the poor,
> But the LORD is his refuge.

Facing the imminent advent of judgment, fools turn not to God to implore mercy. Instead, they turn to the righteous remnant with renewed rage. They refuse to give up. Thus, the character of the foolish is fixed. Do not ever play the role! They wish to humiliate the afflicted, but ultimately they will be unable to destroy God's people, because the Lord Himself is their refuge.

Wanting to put the righteous to shame, the poetic justice implied is that the fool himself will be shamed (see Ps. 53:5).[5] The fool is contrasted in this section with the "righteous," those who are as God desires them to be. The righteous ones stand in glaring opposition to the fool, which is what man becomes without God. In the fullest sense, only the Lord Jesus is the truly Righteous One, the total opposition of all that is folly.

Prayer for Vindication

In verse seven of Psalm 14 we find the necessary response on the part of the reader to the two classes of

---

[5]The relationship of Psalm 14 to its doublet Psalm 53 is a difficult problem to solve. It may be that David wrote both poems from a similar standpoint, but for slightly different reasons, and perhaps at different points in his career. Psalm 14 seems to have an emphasis on the comfort of the righteous, whereas Psalm 53 contains an instructive warning to the wicked (contrast 14:5–6 with 53:5).

humanity in this Psalm. God has revealed both universal folly among mankind (vv. 1–3) and the ultimate disaster that awaits those who continue in that folly
(vv. 4–6). Now we hear the words of the prayer of David,
words which become our prayer as well:

> O that the salvation of Israel would come out of Zion!
> When Yahweh restores the fortunes of His people;
>   Jacob will rejoice,
>   Israel will be glad! (v. 7, personal translation).

Here is David's prayer for the end of folly, for the final
deliverance of the people of God, for the full revelation of
the King of glory. These words are the Old Testament
anticipation of the model prayer our Lord gave us during
His earthly ministry: "Your kingdom come, your will be
done on earth as it is in heaven" (Matt. 6:10, NIV).

The complacency of many in our age to the things of
God drives us to pray for the coming of the King and His
kingdom. O that salvation were come out of Zion, we
pray, that the King would be here and His righteousness
would be revealed (see Ps. 53:6). This will be a time for
the gladdening of all of His people. The fortunes of His
people will be restored, the captivity will return, and the
salvation of Israel will be accomplished.

How Should We Then Live?

How should we then live, given the information that
this Psalm presents? We have been made to face the
nasty fact of the universal depravity of mankind. We
have been made to confront the horrifying notion of the
ultimate judgment that awaits those who do not know
Christ. How *should* we live who know Him?

First, *we should be discerning.* It is by God's grace we
are who we are. But we need to be constantly aware of
the "prince of the power of the air" who is very active
among the fools of this age (see Eph. 2:1–3). We must
keep our hearts soft toward Christ and His people. The

activity of folly is all about us. The same grace of God that has rescued us can also preserve us from folly encroaching into our life-style. We should *not* be duped.

Second, *we should be grateful.* It is by God's grace that we are no longer among those who continue to walk in the folly of their ways. This is not of our own doing; it is all of God. As Paul writes so movingly in Ephesians:

> Also we all once conducted ourselves in the lusts of our flesh, fulfilling the desires of the flesh and of the mind, and were by nature children of wrath, just as the others. But God, who is rich in mercy, because of His great love with which He loved us, even when we were dead in trespasses, made us alive together with Christ (by grace you have been saved) (Eph. 2:3–5).

Praise *is* a matter of life and breath. We who have the life of the Lord Jesus are bound to use our very breath to magnify His grace and thank Him.

There is no room in the Christian community for a feeling of superiority over the foolish that surround us, for such were we—and would be still—save by the grace of God!

Third, *we should be compassionate.* Just as we once walked in the ways of folly but were brought to a knowledge of true wisdom in the Lord Jesus Christ, so there are many about us living in folly whom the Lord might use us to rescue. A biblical view of man in the light of Psalm 14 is not a call for complacency toward fools. Rather, this text demands a renewed commitment to be used by God to compassionately rescue fools from their folly.[6]

Fourth, *we should instruct our families in wisdom.* Our children are growing up in a world of increasing

---

[6]For wise ways to reach the fools you know for Jesus see Joseph C. Aldrich, *Life-Style Evangelism: Crossing Traditional Boundaries to Reach the Unbelieving World* (Portland: Multnomah, 1981).

hostility to the things of God and a general complacency to His being central in the scheme of things. If ever there was a need for Christian parents to seize every opportunity to teach their children, it is in this the age of expectation. We are familiar with the words of Deuteronomy 6:6–7, the command to teach one's children diligently and creatively. Now we need to *do* it. "Do it?" As Becky Manley Piepert observes, fools think that to be "tacky." But it must be done!

The only way to oppose folly in our homes is by constant and innovative teaching of the things that speak of God. This teaching needs to be done with dependence upon the Spirit of God and with a great sense of love and sensitivity to the children.

Remember! God has not given us prophecy of future judgment such as we find in Psalm 14 merely to satisfy our curiosity. He has given us these prophetic words as a gift to help us order our lives better and to affect our world for Him.

Punkin under the Pear Tree

Sometimes we miss the most exquisite opportunities to proclaim the name of the Lord in our homes and among our children just because we are not alert to them. Not long ago I nearly missed such an opportunity, but was spared the loss by the good advice of my wife, Beverly.

When our daughter Rachel was in the early and difficult stages of her battle with leukemia,[7] there was a period of time in which she would hardly respond to anyone or anything. The one exception, we found, was dogs. The sound of a dog's bark or the sight of a dog

---

[7]The story of Rachel's escape from death in the course of this disease is given by the writer in *Praise! A Matter of Life and Breath* (Nashville: Nelson, 1980), Chapter 15.

through the window was always something that elicited a response from her, no matter how weak she was.

My sister gave Rachel a puppy on her second birthday, a day that followed shortly after Rachel came into remission. This little nondescript dog became our daughter's source of comfort as well as the constant companion of her brother. Bruce named the puppy for his sister. He called him "Punkin," a pet name one of Rachel's doctors used. How they loved him!

Three years passed. Then came the day we feared. Despite our attempts to change his habit, Punkin would often go into the road and chase a car. One day a car chased back. Rachel and Bruce lost their dog. Punkin was dead.

My first thought was to bury him quietly and then to tell the children later—a disastrous plan! Beverly's wisdom prevailed, and we had a "funeral service" for our little dog.

Please understand we were not engaging in nonsense. Punkin was not a "Christian dog." But we are a Christian family who seized an opportunity to magnify the name of God in a time of stress.

Out in the orchard, beneath a large pear tree, we dug a hole. Then we brought the inert form of Punkin and talked of his life and death.

Rachel had cried earlier in the house. Bruce had resolved not to cry. I told the children that we would now put Punkin in the ground. "No!" Rachel said. "Him will get cold and wet and dirty. Can't we take him to the hospital?" But it was death we had to face. Over and over we had to explain that Punkin was dead.

"Can I hug him once more?" she asked. Both children hugged their Punkin. Then we buried him there under the pear tree, all helping to pat the cold dirt, all of us awash with tears.

And we prayed. We thanked the Lord for the happiness that Punkin's life had brought us. We expressed our grief to the Lord at the loss his death presented. And then we thanked the Lord that if we were soon to die, our destiny would be quite unlike that of our puppy under the pear tree. While his remains will help the pears to grow, our lives will be ruled by Jesus. While Punkin's flesh will decompose and even his bones will decay, we expect the resurrection of our bodies in newness of life.

Days later Rachel, who has given much thought to death in her young life, whispered these words to me before her good-night hug. "Thank you, Daddy, for letting me help put Punkin in the cold ground. Thank you for telling me that in heaven *we* will not feel cold and wet and all dirty." Thank You, Lord, for not letting us miss this opportunity to make proclamation of Your name in our family.

I know of no more important response to the dreadful teaching of Psalm 14 than to be actively at work combating folly and foolishness. A great deal of that work should be done within our own families.

The facts of Psalm 14 are harsh facts. The fate of the fool is occasioned by his failure to relate the reality of God to his daily life. This is a fate to be avoided! *There is no new song for the fool.* To learn the new song of the Savior-King, we fools had to abandon our folly.

And for now, we continue to sing the new song of the rule of Christ in our own lives and add our "Amen" to the prayer of both Psalms and seers:

Even so, come, Lord Jesus!

Third Movement

Here Comes the King!

"We shall also find that there
is a biblical music of prophecy
that is martial and strident,
with harsh harmonies—all drums
and brass. Here we shall look
at Psalms 2, 110, and 97."

Even So, Come!
Lord Jesus

Let's have another interlude. It has bothered me for years that the Book of Revelation concludes as it does. The beginning of Revelation is itself curious enough. Here is a book with so many figures of speech, images, and pictures that even the angels must debate its meaning! And Revelation begins with a promised blessing to those who read it (see Rev. 1:3). It is the only book of the Bible to grant such a stimulus up front. But look at how Revelation ends:

> He who testifies to these things says, "Surely I am coming quickly." Amen. Even so, come, Lord Jesus! (Rev. 22:20).

Just before the benediction (v. 21) we hear the words of the Savior that He is soon to come, and the words of the seer follow saying "Yes."

Sometimes the words of John are taken too lightly. The manner in which we banter about the word *Maranatha!* in the sense "Our Lord, come" is at times too casual.[1]

---

[1]The word *Maranatha!* is found in the Bible in 1 Corinthians 16:22. It is an Aramaic word comprised of the elements *Maran* or *Marana,* "our Lord," and *tha* or *atha,* "come." The word may have had its origin in the celebration of the Eucharist. It can be translated three ways: (1) "Our Lord has come" (in the incarnation); (2) "Our Lord has come" (in the Eucharist); and (3) "Our Lord, come!" (in the kingdom to come). See R. Nicole, "Maranatha" in *The Zondervan Pictorial Encyclopedia of the Bible,* ed. Merrill C. Tenney, 5 vols. (Grand Rapids: Zondervan, 1975), vol. 4, pp. 70–71.

Have we really read the words of Revelation in the sense that the Apostle John intended? Listen to the full wording of the blessing that attends the reading of his book:

> Blessed is he who reads and those who hear the words of this prophecy, and keep those things which are written in it; for the time is near (Rev. 1:3).

That is, we are not to read once over lightly. The blessing comes when we read and take to heart and act upon what these pages present. It is only such a one who receives the blessing the Spirit promises. It is only such a one who rightly says, "Even so, come! Lord Jesus."

When we say "Come!" to Jesus the King, we are affirming that we are spiritually prepared for the coming period of disaster that will fall upon the world. John exhausts pictorial representations of these calamities by visions of seals, bowls, and trumpets.

It *is* necessary to join John in his expectation of the coming of the King. The kingdom *will be* glorious, and the rule of King Jesus *will be* blessed forever.

But getting there from here will not be pleasant! Do you sometimes feel that song is sour in your everyday life? Wait for a bowl or two; listen for just a couple of trumpets!

For a fresh view of the distresses of the end times, read Psalms 2, 110, and 97. These poems will keep us singing, but there is a martial ring to the new music of these texts that seems foreign to the praise we wish to give the Prince of Peace.

As we begin to hear the music we hear the sound of drums and brass. The King *is* coming—as Judge!

CHAPTER 9

As the Drums Begin to Roll

Psalm 2

Yea, amen, let all adore thee,
  High on thine eternal throne;
Saviour, take the power and glory,
  Claim the kingdom for thine own:
    Alleluia!
Thou shalt reign, and thou alone!

—Charles Wesley

If in the past you have thought of the Psalms as sweet poems which say nice things about God, Psalm 2 will present a difficulty. For in our study of this Psalm, we will find that the drums of end-time prophecy begin to roll. And it is not a pretty sound.

In his splendid novel, *My Name Is Asher Lev*,[1] Chaim Potok presents the development of genius in an artist who grows up in Brooklyn, the son of a traditional, Hasidic Jewish family. Asher Lev's mother is a darkly troubled, brooding woman who feebly attempts to respond to the creative, but unexpected, gift in her son by asking him to paint pictures of pretty flowers. Asher's growing estrangement from his family is occasioned in part by his inability merely to draw pictures of sentimental prettiness when his artistic vision is focused on pain, turmoil, and torment.

Similarly, there would be no integrity in a poem of the

---

[1]Chaim Potok, *My Name Is Asher Lev* (New York: Knopf, 1972).

coming final battle if pain were masked, turmoil ignored, and torment dismissed. This is no time for pretty flowers. Psalm 2 is a war chant as forces are mustered together for the impending battle of Armageddon.[2]

In Time

In our study of Psalm 93 we found it necessary to learn something about Canaanite poetry and thought. In order to understand Psalm 2, we need to learn something about the theology of the kingdom in Israel as rooted in the covenant God made with David (see 2 Sam. 7).

At the time God established this covenant, David had been given rest by the Lord from all of his enemies. David was living in a fine palace, but the Ark of the Covenant—the symbol of the abiding presence of the Lord—was still in a tent. David's desire was to build a temple for the ark. Nathan the prophet, operating on his own, gave David permission to proceed. But then the prophet received a revelation from Yahweh that David was *not* to build the house he desired. Rather, the Lord was going to build a house for David—a house of posterity rather than of stone.

A study of the Davidic covenant brings one to the heart of Old Testament theology. For our present purposes we will only examine the verses that relate directly to the interpretation of the second Psalm. These are the crucial words of God to His beloved servant David:

"I will be his Father, and he shall be My son. If he commits iniquity, I will chasten him with the rod of men and with the blows of the sons of men. But My mercy shall not

---

[2]The New Testament attributes this Psalm to David (see Acts 4:25). It is surprising that this Psalm does not have a superscription in the Old Testament.

depart from him, as I took it from Saul, whom I removed from before you. And your house and your kingdom shall be established forever before you. Your throne shall be established forever" (2 Sam. 7:14–16).

These verses present God's plan for the Davidic line in an extraordinary manner. There will be no "Plan B." Unlike the trial, failure, and rejection of Saul as king, the Davidic line would endure in perpetuity.[3] The issue of sin would be dealt with severely on a case-by-case basis. But the ongoing loyal love of God would never cease from the House of David.

David's friend Ethan sang along the same lines as he responded to the Davidic covenant in Psalm 89. Ethan quotes from 2 Samuel 7 in these poetic words:

"I have made a covenant with My chosen,
I have sworn to My servant David:
    'Your seed I will establish forever,
    And build up your throne to all generations'"
(Ps. 89:3–4).

Adopted by God

Along the way each descendant of David would be adopted by God according to the words of the covenant: "I will be his Father, and he shall be My son" (2 Sam. 7:14). We may presume that these words were used by the priests as each new king was crowned as the successor of David. As an adoptive "son" of God, the king was God's regent on earth, marked out to mediate the divine will among his subjects.

Regent College professor Bruce K. Waltke writes:

---

[3]The contrasting stories of Saul and David are presented in an accessible format by J. Carl Laney, *First and Second Samuel* (Chicago: Moody, 1982).

Now it is important to note that each living successor to David's throne was clothed in the large, magnificent, purple mantle of the messianic vision attached to the House of David. Each king became the son of God through his anointing with Yahweh's Spirit.[4]

Each king in the line of David was regarded as a son of God in the adoptive words of Psalm 2:7, "You are My son,/Today I have begotten you."[5]

Ultimate Fulfillment

In the Lord Jesus Christ the words of Psalm 2 find their ultimate fulfillment. Each king in the Davidic line had his place in these words, but *the* fulfillment which fills all is in the person of Christ. Waltke concludes, "Jesus of Nazareth, Son of David and Son of God, fulfills these psalms."[6]

A thousand years after David's promise, a line never lacking in male issue results in the birth of David's greatest son. Significantly (in terms of the covenant), this One does not marry and has no male issue. For this Son succeeds Himself! By His resurrection, the Lord Jesus Christ is the eternal King to whom will come all the promises of God.

It is significant that Paul quotes Psalm 2:7 as realized in Jesus by the fact of His resurrection:

---

[4]Bruce K. Waltke, "A Canonical Process Approach to the Psalms," in John S. Feinberg and Paul D. Feinberg, eds., *Tradition and Testament: Essays in Honor of Charles Lee Feinberg* (Chicago: Moody, 1981), p. 14. Waltke quotes Helmer Ringgren to the same effect: "The king is Anointed of Yahweh, he is set up by him and proclaimed his son." *The Messiah in the Old Testament* (Chicago: Allenson, 1956), p. 20.

[5]The NKJV reads the word "son" as "Son," which is ultimately correct as the Psalm finds fulfillment in Christ. In the line of David leading up to Christ the word should be in the lower case. For a similar statement of this point of view, see Derek Kidner, *Psalms 1–72* (Downers Grove, Ill.: Inter-Varsity, 1973), p. 51. He states that a coronation rite is suggested by the word *today,* "to mark the moment when the new sovereign formally took up his inheritance and his titles."

[6]Waltke, "Canonical Process," p. 16.

"And we declare to you glad tidings—that promise which was made to the fathers. God has fulfilled this for us their children, in that He has raised up Jesus. As it is also written in the second Psalm:

'You are My Son,
Today I have begotten You'"

(Acts 13:32–33).[7]

There are thus two ways in which the Scriptures speak of Jesus as the "Son of God." In the context of the doctrine of the Trinity, the Lord Jesus Christ is the *eternal* Son of God, blessed forever. There was never a time He did not exist, for He as eternally begotten of the Father has always shared fully in the divine nature.

In the context of the doctrine of the kingdom and the House of David, however, the Lord Jesus Christ, the eternal Son of God, becomes the *incarnate* Son of God in the Davidic sense of 2 Samuel 7:14 and Psalm 2:7.[8] The Son of God assumed human nature in the womb of His mother, Mary.

The Raging Nations

As we now turn to Psalm 2 we find that it has four movements, each composed of three verses. In the first movement we observe *the raging of the nations as they defy Yahweh and His Messiah* (vv. 1–3).

---

[7]The writer to the Hebrews quotes this verse also of the resurrection of Christ. The writer uses Psalm 2:7 to prove that when Christ became high priest it was because of the sovereign selection of God (cf. Heb. 5:5; 8:1 ff.). The conjunction of priest and king will be developed in our next chapter.

[8]In no way is the concept we are advancing to be confused with the heresy of "adoption," whereby Jesus is said not to be eternally the Son of God, but is said to have become such at some point in His lifetime. This was the subject of considerable discussion between the writer and New Testament scholar Dr. Merrill C. Tenney (October 1975, Portland, Oregon). On the other hand, we question some uses traditionally made of Psalm 2:7 to support the correct doctrine of the eternal procession of Jesus as the Son of God. One example is Augustus Hopkins Strong, *Systematic Theology: A Compendium* (Reprint ed., Westwood, N. J.: Revell, 1963), p. 340.

Why do the nations rage,
And the people plot a vain thing?
The kings of the earth set themselves,
And the rulers take counsel together,
Against the LORD and against His Anointed, saying,
"Let us break Their bonds in pieces
And cast away Their cords from us."

When we read these words, we may think first of their setting in the history of Israel. In the career of each descendant of David there was the potential of assault by foreign kings. These verses in Psalm 2:1–3 would relate in a general way to the folly of such an attack. This would be true, providing that the king was rightly relating himself to God and was living in a manner in keeping with the covenant provisions. Given the conditions of faithfulness in the House of David, such situations would not occur with much regularity!

We know that the monarchy eventually collapsed in the Babylonian conquest of 587–586 B.C. by Nebuchadnezzar. This was the ultimate chastening that was fully in accord with the provisions of the covenant (see 2 Sam. 7:14). Nevertheless, *the covenant itself goes on.* As Dr. Charles Ryrie of Dallas Seminary observes, this was attested to by Jeremiah even in the *darkest* days of Judah's decline.[9]

They Raged in Jesus' Day and Will Rage Again

Not only did the nations gather to rage against the king in Judah on many occasions in the time of the monarchy, but they also raged against the Son of David in the life of our Lord. When the enemies of the Lord Jesus conspired for His arrest and eventual death, the ulti-

---

[9]Charles Caldwell Ryrie, *The Basis of the Premillennial Faith* (New York: Loizeaux, 1953), quotes from Jeremiah 23:5–6; 30:8–9; 33:14–17, 20, 21 (pp. 86–87). This point is also made very strongly in Psalm 89.

mate emptiness of their actions was predicted in the words of Psalm 2:1–3.

This is the major point of Acts 4:23–30. When Peter and John rehearsed their experience before the Sanhedrin, the people responded by quoting from Psalm 2:1–2. They then explained:

> For truly against Your holy Servant Jesus, whom You anointed, both Herod and Pontius Pilate, with the Gentiles and the people of Israel, were gathered together to do whatever Your hand and Your purpose determined before to be done (Acts 4:27–28).

The raging of the nations against the kings of Judah was sporadic, limited in scope and duration. The raging of the nations against the person of the Lord has been monumental. But even the raging of the Herods and Pilates of history has been limited compared to the way the nations will rage as they sense the second advent of our Lord drawing near.

In many prophecies of the Old and New Testaments there are descriptions of the final conflict between good and evil, between the Lord and Satan, between Christ and the nations. Our Lord described this period of time as unparalleled in the history of the earth (see Matt. 24:21–22). This day of false expectations and misguided hope (v. 23), of deception and deceit (vv. 24–26), of carnage and distress (vv. 28–29) will be followed by the great event that ends history, begins the kingdom, and ushers in eternity: the glorious return of Christ to the earth. Here are the words of the Savior, the coming King.

> "Immediately after the tribulation of those days the sun will be darkened, and the moon will not give its light; the stars will fall from heaven, and the powers of the heavens will be shaken. Then the sign of the Son of Man will appear in heaven, and then all the tribes of the earth will

mourn, and they will see the Son of Man coming on the clouds of heaven with power and great glory. And He will send His angels with a great sound of a trumpet, and they will gather together His elect from the four winds, from one end of heaven to the other" (Matt. 24:29–31).

In these words we see that the terrible end of this age will be followed by the glorious appearance of the Lord Jesus to begin His rule of light and joy. We expect, then, that the worst will precede the best.[10]

David Saw That Day

We are not surprised to read of the end of the age in the teaching of our Lord or in the visions of the seer John. But we may be surprised indeed to learn that a millennium before the time of Jesus and John, David saw the same things and wrote poems to describe them, poems which became part of the worship music of the temple. In Psalm 2:1–2 David speaks of the raging of the nations that will align themselves to confront the re-turning Christ.

The words of Psalm 2:1–2 are descriptive of the align-ment of the nations to destroy the rule of God on this earth. It is the latter day mirror image of the folly of the people who struggled to build the tower of Babel (see Gen. 11:1–9). In that primeval action, all peoples were united together in common cause against God. The di-vine judgment in that age was confusion of language and, we may presume, differentiation of nations, races, and the beginnings of individual cultures.

Since that event on the rim of human history, peoples have been kept apart from any truly united effort by their own diversities. There are two major ways for dis-parate peoples to come together. One is as peoples of all

---

[10]See Charles C. Ryrie, *The Best Is Yet to Come* (Chicago: Moody, 1981), p. 29.

racial and cultural backgrounds become one in the Body of Christ, the church (see Eph. 2:11–22).

The other way in which the nations will come together is to attempt to destroy the power of Christ. It is this latter action of which David speaks prophetically in Psalm 2:3, "Let us break Their bonds in pieces / And cast away Their cords from us." In these arrogant words the nations rage and mumble; they gather and station themselves to ward off the God of heaven and His Messiah.

God's Perspective

Psalm 2 presents the divine perspective of the folly of the nations as they gather together at the end of the age to make war on the Lord. In Revelation 19:19, John gives the New Testament revelation that corresponds to Psalm 2: "And I saw the beast, the kings of the earth, and their armies, gathered together to make war against Him who sat on the horse and against His army."

But they rage in vain! The use of the parallel terms "nations" and "the people" in Psalm 2:1 speaks of the comprehensive alignment of world rulers led by the bestial one to forestall the Lord's Messiah.

The verbs in the verse carry forth the action well. The verb "rage" is a particularly strong term of collective tumult. The Arabic cognate to this Hebrew word means "to make a vehement noise." This strong verb is balanced by a softer verb, "to muse, meditate, mumble." This verb is in fact the very same verb used in Psalm 1:2b of the believer meditating on the law of the Lord. In this word of mumbling vanities against the Lord, we have something of a parody of the delight and mumblings of the righteous over the Word of God.

And Then He Laughs

Those who are leading these sordid deliberations are the potentates of the nations at the time of the final battle. For the first time since the building of the tower of Babel, rulers of the world and their subjects will be united in defying the Almighty. In both instances, their chances for success are nil.

Nonetheless, they will take their stand and counsel together in solemn conclave to withstand Yahweh and His Messiah. So the forces all gather together . . . and God *quakes*. He quakes, not in fear, but in gales of derisive laughter!

In the second section of Psalm 2 we read of *the scorn of the Father as He reasserts His program.*

> He who sits in the heavens shall laugh;
> The LORD shall hold them in derision.
> Then He shall speak to them in His wrath,
> And distress them in His deep displeasure:
> "Yet I have set My King
> On My holy hill of Zion" (Ps. 2:4–6).

On occasion in the pages of the Bible we read of God's laughing in pleasure with His people. But Psalm 2:4 speaks of another kind of laugh. Here is a laugh of sarcastic scorn—a dreadful, mocking laugh. This is a laugh that is an adequate response to the preposterous claim that a man might successfully defy God. The words, "Don't make me laugh," said by countless schoolboys as they measure each other like cocks about to fight, are here magnified to inestimable proportions.

This scornful laughing of God against His foes is not unparalleled in the Bible. Wisdom shares such a bitter laugh in Proverbs 1:26 as she predicts the destruction that will come to those who choose folly instead of the insight she offers. They will get what they deserve, and she will mock them in their calamitous end.

Each time God defeats the foes of His kings, He laughs at His enemies. This is the conclusion of David in Psalm 59:8.

But You, O Lord, shall laugh at them;
You shall have all the nations in derision.

The reason that God *must* laugh is that He *is* King (Ps. 59:13, "And let them know that God rules in Jacob / To the ends of the earth"). In Psalm 2 we hear God's last, bitter laugh.

The Determination of the Father

As the first movement of Psalm 2 ended in a prophetic quotation of the wicked world rulers, stating their purposes, so the second movement of the Psalm ends in a prophetic quotation of the King of glory, giving His purposes: "For I am determined to install My King / upon Zion, My holy hill" (Ps. 2:6, personal translation). The verb here appears to be a perfect of resolve, stating the strong determination of Yahweh to install His King in Zion. This rare verb (used only here and in Proverbs 8:23) is buttressed by the strong personal pronoun, "For I" or "But as for Me." This wording gives more emphasis to the determination of the Lord.

At that time there will come upon the nations the full fury of the King of glory for their unspeakable arrogance—an arrogance that is all too common in our world. Far too many people have no time for God as King. By their thoughts and their actions they dethrone Him in their minds. To all such ones comes the harsh sound of the laughter of God.

The Promise to the Son

In the third strophe of Psalm 2 we read of *the promise* of the Father to the Son of His sure rule:

"I will declare the decree:
The LORD has said to Me,

'You are My Son,
Today I have begotten You.
Ask of Me, and I will give You
The nations for Your inheritance,
And the ends of the earth for Your possession.
You shall break them with a rod of iron;
You shall dash them in pieces like a potter's vessel'"
(Ps. 2:7–9).

In verse seven of Psalm 2 there is a change of speakers. The Son Himself is speaking and He quotes the words of the Father respecting Himself. This Psalm is truly holy ground; for in this poem of David we have the innercommunication of the triune Deity.

The vocabulary and style of verse seven is elevated and solemn. The word for speaking, "I will declare," "I will now rehearse," is a fairly unusual term. We are also struck by the term "decree." The Hebrew word ḥôq ("decree") is used in a similar way in Psalm 105:10–11, concerning God's covenant with Abraham granting him the land of Palestine. The term is used also in a decree of the Lord's anger by the prophet Zephaniah (2:1–2).

The Great Decree

The decree mentioned in Psalm 2:7 is the covenant God made with David in 2 Samuel 7, just as the decree of Psalm 105:10 is the covenant God made with Abraham in Genesis 12. The King-Priest who is our Messiah now gives the words of the Father concerning the kingdom that He is to win. As the nations are gathering their standards, marshaling their troops, and making their plans (vv. 1–3), there are some plans being made in heaven as well!

All that the Son needs to do is ask the Father and He will receive all nations as His heritage. This great text (Ps. 2:8) speaks of the sovereignty of the Father, of the eternal rule of God, and of the fully expected realization of the future rule of Jesus Christ on earth. God's purpose is clear: He is determined to set His King on His holy hill, Zion.

The words of verse nine speak of breaking the enemies with a rod of iron and dashing God's foes as clay pots. These images are harsh. We may join the mother of Asher Lev and ask for pictures of pretty flowers instead. These concepts hardly fit with the image that many have about sweet Jesus with flowers and doting children. Reality is often like that—surprising and unsettling.

Some of us must wonder if God really will judge the nations with the severity that passages like this suggest. Do we not hear something quite different on television and radio talk shows? Even clerics and religious leaders are uncomfortable with the doctrine of the final judgment.

Perhaps it is *because of* our disinclination to believe in the harsh reality of the coming judgment that our Lord has given us so many prefigurations of it in the Old and New Testaments. We are more inclined to believe in the judgments that are coming as we read the accounts of judgments that came in the past.

It was the God of love who destroyed Sodom, Gomorrah, and the other cities of the valley (see Gen. 19: 23–29). It was the God and Father of the Lord Jesus Christ who brought about havoc and ruin on the cities of Jericho and Hazor (see Josh. 6, 11).

An Endangered Species

Moreover, it was our Lord who brought about the destruction of the antediluvian world because of rampant sinfulness (see Gen. 6–9). And this primeval destruction in the flood is to be taken as a positive indicator that God is as serious about the coming judgment as He was about past judgment. Peter uses the paradigm of judgment in the past to guarantee the coming judgment (see 2 Pet. 3:5–8).

God no more asked permission in the past for the judgment He brought upon the earth in the flood than He will ask permission in the future for the judgment that is to come. The fire will come next time.

The most seriously endangered species of life on this planet is the species of wicked men. No congressional bill or ecological action committee shall be able to help save this species. One day God will say, "Enough is enough!" Then the drums of heaven will begin to roll. Psalm 110 has the trumpets playing as well.

Instructions from the Spirit

Psalm 2 is truly an extraordinary passage. It is a poem that was used in countless worship services in ancient Israel as the community of faith renewed their allegiance to the rule of God as expressed through their God-given king. It contains the ideal that was set before each of these kings: live as the son of God and His regent upon this earth. But most importantly, it contains the specific prophecy of the coming rule of King Jesus.

This Psalm is remarkable in terms of the speakers as well. In the first strophe, the speaker is David as he reflects on the irrational evil of rulers and world leaders (vv. 1–3). In the second strophe, the speaker is God the Father. All heaven rocks with His laughter at the arrogance of wicked men (vv. 4–6). In the third strophe we hear the words of the son (each king, the ideal king, and the final King), who is ultimately the Son of God Himself and who reports the words of the Father on His behalf (vv. 7–9).

In the fourth strophe (vv. 10–12) we hear the words of the Spirit in solemn warning to all earthly leaders of the reality of the rule of God, both in the present and in the future. God *is* King. The rule on earth of the heavenly King is coming. None shall stand against Him, not one!

Wise Up!

Here are the words of the fourth strophe of Psalm 2:

> Now therefore, be wise, O kings;
> Be instructed, you judges of the earth.
> Serve the LORD with fear,
> And rejoice with trembling.
> Kiss the Son, lest He be angry,
> And you perish in the way,
> When His wrath is kindled but a little.
> Blessed are all those who put their trust in Him
> (Ps. 2:10–12).

The prophetic Scriptures were not given as puzzles for us to study on cold winter nights. The texts explain their own reasons for being. These texts help us to "wise up" concerning the desperate nature of sin, the one thing that can preclude our participation in the rule of God and His Messiah.

Listen to the words of Peter concerning the practical results of the doctrine of future judgment:

> Therefore, since all these things will be dissolved, what manner of persons ought you to be in holy conduct and godliness, looking for and hastening the coming of the day of God, because of which the heavens will be dissolved being on fire, and the elements will melt with fervent heat? (2 Pet. 3:11–12).

These strong encouragements to holy living are followed by commands to "be diligent to be found by Him in peace, without spot and blameless" (v. 14), to "beware lest you also fall from your own steadfastness, being led away with the error of the wicked" (v. 17), and to "grow in the grace and knowledge of our Lord and Savior Jesus Christ" (v. 18).

Worship Him!

To the enemies of the living Christ come the commands that they worship Him, serve Him, submit to Him fully, and rejoice in Him rightly (Ps. 2:11–12). What demands these are, given the ones addressed!

Yet, you and I are also addressed by these words. For these commands are as proper in their application to our own lives as they are to the kings of the earth in all ages. The drums have begun to roll. Soon, so will the heads!

It is most impressive to me that in this Psalm of coming judgment there is such an impassioned appeal for men to worship the Lord. Verse 11 presents a strongly balanced picture of the worship of God and His Christ. The verbs for worshiping ("serve" and "rejoice") are both modified by terms of fear and reserve:

> Serve Yahweh in piety,
> And rejoice in trembling!
> (Ps. 2:11, personal translation).

The fear of the Lord and the adoration of the Lord are not contrary actions, but complementary. The Lord in whom we rejoice is the *Lord*. Many are they who in their joy in the Lord forget that He is *Lord*. This is a balance most difficult to maintain.

I suspect that in the course of time the church has gone back and forth from one side of the picture to the other. At times we have been too fearful of God and at other times far too familiar. This great text balances awe and piety on one hand and rejoicing service on the other. The "fear and trembling" elements are necessary correlates to the "serve and rejoice" aspects. God desires a balance from His people in these areas of response to Himself.

Although not without its difficulties, most translations of the Bible render the beginning words of verse 12 as "Kiss the Son." Our problem is not with the word "kiss," but with an unexpected term for "Son." The word for "Son" used earlier in the poem is the Hebrew word *bēn* (v. 7). The term in verse twelve is *bar,* a rare term for "son" in Hebrew, but more common in Aramaic. Some scholars have suggested that the latter word may be taken as an adverb meaning "purely" and that the command is to give to the enthroned One "sincere homage."[11]

Whether we translate "kiss the Son" or "kiss with sincerity," the meaning of this verse is clear enough. There are two options available to the kings of the earth and their subjects. These are the same two options that we have today. Either we can submit joyfully to the rule of the Lord, or we can oppose His rule. There appears to be no middle ground in the mind of God. The gurus of our age likely cherish some vague middle way—but there is none. God *is* King. Jesus is the *coming* King.

To those who chose to oppose Him there is the haunting laughter of God, followed by the sure and certain wrath before which heaven will blush. To those who honor Him and own Him as King, there is an abundant blessing of hope and certainty. Psalm 2 ends as Psalm 1 began, with a beatitude of blessing on the righteous. At last we will get the pictures of pretty flowers; but the beauty will be in truth, not in sentiment alone.

The drums have begun to roll. David heard them in Psalm 2. In Psalm 110 he heard the trumpets and the battle sounds as well.

Our Refuge

For those of us who know the Savior and, like Ruth, have taken refuge under His wings (cf. Ruth 2:12), the last words of this Psalm are a comfort.

---

[11]See Kidner, *Psalms 1–72,* pp. 52–53. The varied versional evidences are presented in critical commentaries. I myself am loath to leave the translation "Son," as the Psalm certainly conditions us to think in such terms (see NIV, NKJV).

O how manifestly happy
  are all those who take refuge in Him!
  (Ps. 2:12d, personal translation).

Charles Coffin (1676–1749) rhapsodized on these thoughts in this way:

> For thou art our salvation, Lord,
>   Our refuge and our great reward;
> Without thy grace we waste away
>   Like flowers that wither and decay.
>
> All praise, eternal Son, to thee
>   Whose advent sets thy people free,
> Whom with the Father we adore,
>   And Holy Ghost, for evermore!

The drums have begun to roll. But do you also hear the strings . . . of praise?

CHAPTER 10

A Hymn of Glory

Psalm 110

A hymn of glory let us sing,
New hymns throughout the world shall ring;
By a new way none ever trod
Christ mounteth to the throne of God,
Christ mounteth to the throne of God.

—THE VENERABLE BEDE, A.D. 673–735

In the Japanese coastal city of Tateyama there is a new shrine for Buddhist pilgrims. As a testimonial of her faith and piety, a very wealthy Japanese philanthropist contributed one million dollars toward making the largest statue of Buddha in the world. The immense bronze statue weighs thirty tons. The Buddha is reclining on his right side, the epitome of escape, of the achievement of enlightenment, of nirvana attained. The Buddha is also asleep.

The mind of man has developed innumerable attempts to enable one to escape the sufferings of life. For some the goal is escape and rest, a cessation of the endless cycle of rebirth to more troubles. So the Buddha is sleeping, and millions of weary pilgrims will watch his slumbering form and wonder if they too will ever find the escape for which they long. The Buddha is asleep.

What a contrast is our Lord Jesus Christ! Our Lord is not asleep! The most vivid image of Christ in His present work is not one of quiet repose, but one of active relationship to His people and interrelationship within the Trinity. The picture the Bible presents most often of our Lord is one of Him seated. Psalm 110:1 reads, "The LORD said to my Lord, / 'Sit at My right hand, / Till I make Your enemies Your footstool.'"

A Seated Lord

Seated He is, but not reclining, not dozing, not relaxing. In one sense He is resting from the work that He did in His incarnation, for the sacrificial acts of the Lord Jesus were done once for all; they are nonrepeatable actions. "He entered the Most Holy Place once for all, having obtained eternal redemption" (Heb. 9:12).

The priests of the Old Testament period were appointed by God for His service. The prime characterization of their work is that it was never over. When one sacrifice would be completed, preparations would be made for the next one. Like the washing of dishes, sacrifice was never over.

But when our Lord offered Himself as the sacrifice to end the sacrificial system, and to bring to fulfillment all of the intentions of God in the worship patterns of Israel, He made all further blood sacrifice sacrilege. And so He sat down!

> Now this is the main point of the things we are saying: We have such a High Priest, who is seated at the right hand of the throne of the Majesty in the heavens (Heb. 8:1).

A Seated King

But there is something else concerning the *seated Lord* we must say. First, His sitting is not passive, but active. Second, His sitting is not simple, but complex.

As in the majestic vision that Isaiah had of Yahweh, King of Kings (see Is. 6), the seated One is *active* and dynamic, never static, and certainly never slumbering.

The picture of the sitting Christ is always dynamic and active. The image of our Lord being seated at the right hand of the Majesty is descriptive of His regal position, not of His indolence.

When a king or queen is seated on the throne, it is then that the reign of that monarch begins. He or she is not seated to relax, but rather to *rule*. Thus, our heavenly King, the Lord Jesus Christ, is seated on the throne of His Father and His servant, David, to reign as head over His people, the church. He is active in leading the affairs of His holy nation.

The picture of the seated Christ is *complex* in that it blends at least two pictures, and it involves a major expectation. As the One seated at the right hand of the Father, the Lord Jesus is in a royal position. He is the seated King! The fact that He is seated speaks also of His priestly position. Yet, what an unlikely position for a priest! Priests, like busy housewives, *never* get to sit down. But this one does, and it is on the basis of the fact that He is seated that He demonstrates His superiority over all other priests. His work of redemption is complete. This is the major argument of Hebrews 5–10.

The seated Christ is also a picture that is anticipative:

But this Man, after He had offered one sacrifice for sins forever, sat down at the right hand of God, from that time waiting till His enemies are made His footstool (Heb. 10:12–13).

The sitting of Christ at the right hand of the Father is an act of anticipation on His part of the coming of the kingdom of God on earth, the subjugation of all the nations to Himself, and the beginning of His righteous rule. Today He is active head over one nation, the church. Tomorrow, He will reign over all nations, the world. The sitting of Christ then is not passive, but active. The sitting of Christ at the right hand of Majesty is complex, speaking of His royalty, His priesthood, and His coming rule.

A Returning King

Since there is so much vital doctrine connected to the concept of the Lord Jesus taking His seat beside the Father in glory, it remains a mystery to me why evangelical, Bible-believing churches do not make more of the Ascension of Christ than they do. When is the last time your church observed Ascension Sunday? The festival of the Ascension has splendid teaching values for the community of believers. Those of us in nonliturgical churches lose a great deal as we ignore the values of the church year.[1]

It was on the day of the Ascension that our Lord said of Himself, "All authority has been given to Me in heaven and on earth" (Matt. 28:18). And it was in the manner of the Ascension that the angels promised His return: "This same Jesus, who was taken up from you into heaven, will so come in like manner as you saw Him go into heaven" (Acts 1:11).

The Ascension is the return of the Lord Jesus into heaven to the place of highest honor for our highest good. He is our King in heaven. And from there He will return as the great King over all the earth. Thomas Kelly wrote so well the excitement that ought to come to God's people as they contemplate the Ascension of our Lord:

> Look, ye saints, the sight is glorious,
> See the Man of Sorrows now;

[1]See our chapter, "Planning for Worship," Ronald Allen and Gordon Borror, *Worship: Rediscovering the Missing Jewel* (Portland: Multnomah, 1982), pp. 63–76. We are planning a supplement to encourage free churches to adopt a modified pattern of the church year. Robert E. Webber gives substantial rationale for the church year in his chapter "Worship and Time," *Worship Old and New* (Grand Rapids: Zondervan, 1982), pp. 161–173.

From the fight returned victorious,
  Every knee to him shall bow;
    Crown Him! Crown Him!
    Crown Him! Crown Him!
Crowns become the victor's brow.
Hark, those bursts of acclamation,
  Hark, those loud triumphant chords!
Jesus takes the highest station;
  O what joy the sight affords!
    Crown Him! Crown Him!
    Crown Him! Crown Him!
King of kings, and Lord of lords.

And it all begins in the Psalms, for it is in Psalm 110 that we first read this hymn of glory.

The Favorite Psalm

If a poll were to be taken on the best-loved Psalm in the Bible, I suspect that Psalm 23 might well be the winner today. But if the same poll were taken in the period of the early church, perhaps Psalm 110 would have won. For this brief Psalm is quoted directly or indirectly more often than any other Psalm in the collection by the writers of the New Testament. This is the Psalm that speaks of the Lord Jesus Christ as King and Priest. It also speaks of Him as the coming Judge.

In no Psalm is the matter of authorship so crucial as it is in this one. Most of our Bibles include the superscription, "Of David. A Psalm," just before verse one. In order for us to understand how very important authorship is in this Psalm, let us imagine for a moment that David was not the author.

If David did not write Psalm 110, then we might assume that the poem was written by a priest, a prophet, or a court musician and that the superscription is either mistaken in fact or in translation. If so, when we read the opening words, "The LORD said to my Lord," we would understand that the first word LORD (Yahweh) unmistakably refers to God. But in this case the words "my Lord" would refer to David (or to one of his successors), as addressed by the writer of the poem. The promise of these words, then, would be the gradual triumph of the Davidic kingdom against all its foes and the establishment of a Judean hegemony over the Middle East.

Each successive Davidite might see himself to a lesser or greater degree fulfilling the promise of the first verse. As we have seen in our study of Psalm 2, the *ultimate* realization of this promise is in the person of the Lord Jesus Christ, the ultimate Davidite. Such a realization might be interpreted to be either in the expansion of the church or in the establishment of the future kingdom of God on earth.

Now we should not minimize this type of interpretation of Psalm 110 too quickly. For one thing, this is the dominant view of many scholars today. Further, the promise of this Psalm read in this way is truly significant. By this promise David and his successors are to expect an ultimate victory over all enemies. The king would regard himself as an honored ally of the living God, who would fight for him. Further, by this interpretation, the words "my Lord" could have a double meaning; ultimately they would point to Messiah Jesus.

David Wrote It

Nonetheless, we believe that David is the indisputable author of Psalm 110 and that in his authorship we have something truly stunning. The interpretation which is common today that denies David as the author of the poem fails on three counts: (1) it does not fit contextual logic within the Psalm, (2) it disregards consistency of Davidic authorship suggested by many superscriptions, and (3) it is countered by the explicit statement of the Lord Jesus Himself.[2]

The first two items would better be addressed in a commentary, but I do wish to stress the third: the witness of the Lord Jesus Himself to the authorship of the Psalm. In Matthew 22:42–46 our Lord's argument *depends* on the Davidic authorship of Psalm 110.

In a lull in our Lord's interaction with the Sadducees and the Pharisees, as the common people listened with astonishment (v. 33), Jesus put a question to His inquisitors (Tiger that He was!), saying, "What do you think about the Christ? Whose Son is He?" (Matt. 22:42). Their response came appropriately, "The Son of David" (v. 42).[3]

Jesus then countered with a conundrum that silenced his foes. But His words hang together *only* if the Davidic authorship of Psalm 110 is assured.

> He said to them, "How then does David in the Spirit call Him 'Lord,' saying:
>
>> 'The LORD said to my Lord,
>> "Sit at My right hand,
>> Till I make Your enemies Your footstool" '?
>
> "If David then calls Him 'Lord,' how is He his Son?" (Matt. 22:43–45).

---

[2]A recent defense of Davidic authorship in this and other Psalms attributed to him is given by Donald Glenn in his contribution to the Feinberg *Festschrift*. See his "An Exegetical and Theological Exposition of Psalm 139" in John S. Feinberg and Paul D. Feinberg, *Tradition and Testament: Essays in Honor of Charles Lee Feinberg* (Chicago: Moody, 1981), pp. 166–67.

[3]The sectarians who lived near the Dead Sea at Qumran, and who were responsible for the famous Dead Sea Scrolls, seem to have expected two messiahs (or even three: the Prophet). This is a common, but not unanimous, view of scholars of the Qumran materials. See G. Vermes, *The Dead Sea Scrolls in English*, 2nd ed. (New York: Penguin, 1975), pp. 47–51. Thus, the response of the Jewish leaders to Jesus may not have been as automatic as we might have expected.

To this question not one of his inquisitors dared to venture an answer. To do so would be to fall into the hands of Jesus and then to bow before Him as the very Promised One of God! The crowd looking on loved it! (See Mark 12:37.) The point that Jesus made is possible only if David is incontrovertibly regarded as the author of the Psalm. The stress that our Lord gives to this ("David in the Spirit") suggests an extraordinary dimension of the leading by the Spirit in these words.[4]

Listening in on God!

How would you like to be a silent auditor to the conversations of the leaders of this world? What if you had an extension of the "hot line" in your own home? What we have in Psalm 110 is something of an inside line in heaven itself! We are with David as he is listening to the innercommunication of the Holy Trinity!

In this text we are in the highest heavens. In these words we join David as he experienced the Father speaking to the Son. David was not the one addressed as "my lord" in this text. David is the one who hears the words, and he says "my Lord" as he recognizes the Person in glory to be his own supreme master.

Here are the words of Psalm 110:1 in a personal translation.

> The solemn utterance[5] of Yahweh to my Lord:
>   "Sit at My right hand,
>   until I make Your enemies,
>   a stool for Your feet."

---

[4]Other New Testament notices of Davidic authorship of Psalm 110 include the parallel texts in Mark 12:35–37; Luke 20:41–44; Acts 2:34; Hebrews 1:13.

[5]This Hebrew term used for the speaking of Yahweh to "my Lord" is *ne'um*, a word regularly used in the prophets to refer to a solemn oracle of God. In the original text of Psalm 110:1, this word is first in the line, setting the stage for the strongly prophetic context.

Here is an explicit prophecy of the exaltation of our Lord Jesus Christ to the position of highest honor at the right hand of the Father and the subjugation of all powers under His feet!

Here is a time for celebration! On the basis of the fulfillment of Psalm 110:1 in the Ascension of Jesus, Peter preached, "Therefore let all the house of Israel know assuredly that God has made this Jesus, whom you crucified, both Lord and Christ" (Acts 2:36).

From David's vantage point, Psalm 110:1 stretches far into the future. Logically and theologically this verse cannot refer to Christ before the time of the Incarnation, nor does it speak of the time of Jesus' life on earth. It goes beyond the cross and even beyond the resurrection! It is of the Ascension and the exaltation in heaven of our Lord that this verse speaks so directly. As Paul writes:

Therefore God also has highly exalted Him and given Him the name which is above every name, that at the name of Jesus every knee should bow, of those in heaven, and of those on earth, and of those under the earth, and that every tongue should confess that Jesus Christ is Lord, to the glory of God the Father (Phil. 2:9–11).[6]

David called him "My *Lord*." So do we. And so shall we all!

The High Priest and the Great Priest

In His trial before the high priest Jesus interpreted the words of Psalm 110:1 as speaking of Himself, and He added to these words the words of Daniel 7:13, "One like the Son of Man, / Coming with the clouds of heaven!" The response of the high priest (to the Grand Priest) was

---

[6]Paul uses the idea of Psalm 110:1 in Ephesians 1:20–23; Colossians 3:1; 1 Corinthians 15:24–28. It is also found in Hebrews 1:3; 8:1; 10:12–13; 12:2. What an *amazing* verse of Old Testament poetry!

one of incredulity. If ever a man blasphemed, it was now—unless Jesus spoke truth!

The high priest tore his robes—an extraordinary act, given their cost. Believing Jesus to be in error, the error was judged to be a capital offense. Those present spat on Him, beat Him, slapped Him, and mocked Him. But they did not listen to Him, nor did they believe Him (see Matt. 26: 63–68).

But for those of us who *do* listen to Him and who *do* believe in Him—what wonder these words have! David heard these words spoken by the Father to the Son. We hear them repeated by the Son concerning His own certain exaltation and glory. Dare we remain unmoved by the message of these words? To these words there must come from us a response of praise. Truly, "praise from the upright is beautiful" (Ps. 33:1).

You and I need to respond to these words in great praise to the exalted and magnified person of Jesus Christ. Our worship services should reflect the majesty and dignity of these words. Our lives should adorn our praise to our exalted Lord. It is to this end that the eternal purposes of God are directed. And we read about these words first in the Psalms of Israel!

> May our affections thither tend,
> And thither constantly ascend,
> Where, seated on the Father's throne,
> Thee reigning in the heavens, we own!
> Thee reigning in the heavens, we own!
>
> —THE VENERABLE BEDE

A Priest Forever

The second great revelation of Psalm 110 is found in verse four:

> The LORD has sworn
> And will not relent,

"You are a priest forever
According to the order of Melchizedek" (Ps. 110:4).

The solemnity and significance of these words are indicated by the introductory oath of God. He brings Himself under oath in the context of His own immutability. As pagan Balaam unwillingly testified five hundred years before David ever heard these words from the Father: "God is not a man, that He should lie,/Nor a son of man, that He should repent./Has He said, and will He not do it?/Or has He spoken, and will He not make it good?" (Num. 23:19).

By two great factors—that God has sworn and that He cannot change (see Heb. 6:16–18)—we now hear the second revelation of the Father to the Son in this Psalm: "You are priest forever."

"Priest!" But He is King! How can He also be priest? In Israel the king was to be from the House of Judah and the priest from the House of Levi. The explanation is found in the fact that the priesthood of Jesus Christ is not determined by Levitical descent among Aaron's sons, but in an entirely nongenetic manner. He is priest in the manner of Melchizedek.

Just as Melchizedek, the somewhat mysterious patriarch of Salem (see Gen. 14:18–20) was acknowledged by Abraham as a legitimate priest of the Most High God, so the Lord Jesus is an accredited priest of true Deity, apart from the expected genetic credentials for the priesthood of the Old Testament period (see Heb. 7:1–14). The fact that Melchizedek was a king-priest should not be lost on us. In the same manner, Jesus will be King-priest as well.

A substantial portion of the Book of Hebrews (chapters 5–10, with 6 as a parenthesis) is given over to a development of this one verse of Psalm 110. Psalm 110:4 speaks of Jesus as priest forever. The writer to the Hebrews demonstrates that Jesus the Grand Priest is superior to all other priests of the line of Aaron.

One of the major preoccupations of the people at the Qumran settlement was to reassert the rightful place for legitimate priests in an age in which the priesthood had become corrupt and tainted. The much talked about "Temple Scroll" (not yet translated into English) has a major section on the legitimacy of the "right" priests and their duties. But Jesus the Great Priest is superior to *all* other priests of the Aaronic line, or any other line, be they in Jerusalem, Qumran, or Katmandu!

Jesus the Great Priest is now in the heavenlies (see Heb. 4:14; 6:19–20). He was called by God for this high honor, just as Aaron was (see Heb. 5:1–4), and Psalm 110:4 is the specific proof of His call (see Heb. 5:5–10). The superiority of Jesus as the Great High Priest is established by the "power of an endless life" (Heb. 7:15–19), the establishing oath (vv. 20–22), His permanent priesthood (vv. 23–25), and His superior sacrifice (vv. 26–28).[7]

The Surprise of Jesus

King *and* priest! This is the great surprise of Jesus Christ! In the one Man the two offices meet and embrace. In the Incarnate Son we have all the messianic promises of God realized. King He is—at the right hand of the Father. Priest He is, in the manner of Melchizedek, at the right hand of the Father forever.

When we consider verses one and four of Psalm 110 together, we may truly be astounded. Here in one brief compass we have *two* of the principal offices of our Lord. These are given in the context of a nearly unprecedented revelation, as David in a mysterious manner is an atten-

---

[7]This fine analysis is presented by Leon Morris, "Hebrews," in *The Expositor's Bible Commentary*, ed. Frank E. Gaebelein, 12 vols. (Grand Rapids: Zondervan, 1978—), vol 12, pp. 68–73.

dant to the words of the Father to the Son in declaring eternal truths.

But when we have done with these words, we still have not done with this Psalm. Although these are the most often quoted verses of the poem, there are still other verses. These other verses are sometimes neglected. One writer refers to this poem as being of gold and clay. On to the "clay"!

Here are the verses which follow the great declaration of the present reign of the Lord Jesus at the right hand of Majesty:

> The Lord shall send the rod of Your strength
>   out of Zion.
> Rule in the midst of Your enemies!
> Your people shall be volunteers
> In the day of Your power;
> In the beauties of holiness,
>   from the womb of the morning,
> You have the dew of Your youth (Ps. 110:2–3).

Some clay! Why are these verses neglected in the preaching of the church and in the general discussion of this Psalm? Is it that they seem to be incongruous with the serene splendor of verse one, with the picture of the Lord seated at the right hand of the Father? Here neither the Father nor the Son is seated. These words have an unsettling effect.

But there is more to the "clay." Here are the words of verses five to seven, verses which follow the revelation of Jesus as the eternal priest:

> The Lord is at Your right hand;
> He shall execute kings in the day of His wrath.
> He shall judge among the nations,
> He shall fill the places with dead bodies,
> He shall execute the heads of many countries.

He shall drink of the brook by the wayside;
Therefore He shall lift up the head.[8]

Some priest! No wonder these verses are ignored. They hardly seem to flow from the solemn pronouncement of the priesthood of our Savior anymore than do the words of verses two and three from the serene picture of seated majesty. They seem hardly to fit the Psalm at all, unless. . . .

Avenging Judge

Although not fitting the usually neat structures that we often find in the Psalms, there are in fact *three revelations* that David heard from the Father to the Son in Psalm 110: (1) Jesus is the awaiting *King*, seated at the right hand of the Father (v. 1); (2) Jesus is the eternal *Priest*, after the manner of Melchizedek (v. 4); and (3) Jesus is the avenging *Judge*, coming with His army to establish His kingdom (vv. 2–3, 5–7). Seen in this way, these verses seem to flow quite naturally from the teaching of Psalm 2, which we discussed in the last chapter.

The words of verse two contain a third revelatory word from the Father to the Son: "Rule in the midst of Your enemies!" The time of the anticipative waiting of verse one is over in the words of verse two; the time for battle has come. The Lord is now leading the attack on all His foes. He comes with a rod of authority and with a mighty army made up not of mercenaries, conscripts, or draftees, but of those who are "freely willing." The Hebrew word translated "volunteers" (v. 3) is often translated "freewill offerings" (e.g., Lev. 7:16 NIV).

The people that join our Lord in battle are in holy

---

[8]The verses in Psalm 110 that we have quoted here from the NKJV are exceptionally difficult to translate with precision. In the following discussion I shall present (with reserve) my own translation, so as to bring out salient features of this text.

garments ("in the beauties of holiness," v. 3), are as innumerable as the dew of the morning, and are as fresh for battle as though they had sprung from the womb of dawn itself. My personal rendering of verse 3 is as follows:

> Your people are freely willing
> on Your battle day;
> In holy array,
> from the womb of the dawn,
> Your youth are like dew to You.[9]

These words describing the people who make up the army of the Lord evoke memories of the hymn, "Who Is on the Lord's Side?" Although when we sing this hymn we think of witnessing for the Lord, the imagery is of martial conflict and the tune is tellingly titled *Armageddon*!

> Fierce may be the conflict,
> Strong may be the foe,
> But the King's own army
> None can overthrow;
> Round His standard raging,
> Victory is secure,
> For His truth unchanging
> Makes the triumph sure.
> Joyfully enlisting,
> By Thy grace divine,
> We are on the Lord's side—
> Savior, we are Thine!

"Joyfully enlisting" is a fine adaptation of the description of the free and willing armies that will attend the battle of the Lord.

---

[9]In my rendering these words are descriptive of the people of the army of the Lord, and not of the Lord Himself as in the text of the NKJV. Commentaries divide on this issue.

Carnage and Corpses

Try as we might, we cannot make the words of verses 5–7 sound pretty. Let us turn to these words again, this time in a personal translation:

> The Lord is at Your right hand;
> He will shatter kings in the day of His wrath.
>
> He will judge among the nations,
>   He will heap up corpses,
>   He will shatter rulers over the broad earth.
>
> He will drink from the brook by the road,
> Thereupon He will hold high His head.

As I understand these words they describe a day of the wrath of God. The active verbs are words of terrible conflict, carnage, and corpses: He will shatter, He will judge, He will heap up, and He will shatter more. Then, with the bulk of the battle done, the great Warrior stops for a refreshing drink of water (v. 7). Then, with head held high, He proceeds to finish the task.

The battle scenes in the Old Testament often speak of the remnant that gets away (e.g., Is. 16:14). In this battle there will be no remnant; none shall escape. After chiefs and rulers are shattered and their corpses are piled high, the Warrior pauses for a moment, but only for a moment. His head is high—He is not even scratched—and He completes His work.

As we read these words we cannot but wonder, What battle is this? Should we speak of the battles of the kings of Judah, or even of King David, and see these verses fulfilled in them? If we attempt to do that, then what is the possible connection between these verses and verses one and four which speak so clearly and exclusively of the person of Jesus Christ?

If we conclude that these verses do speak of the Lord Jesus, should we brush through them quickly and say that these verses use a military image for the conquest that Christ makes in the hearts of men, that the battlefield is a purely spiritual one? Can such really be the interpretation? Do soul-winners not only "collect scalps," but also "shatter rulers" and "heap up corpses" as well?

Are we not driven by any fair reading of these words to see that the clay in them is in our own eyes? Are we not driven to the description in these words to the scene in the Bible of the last battle, the Battle of Armageddon? Does this text not speak dramatically of the return of Christ to the earth as described by another seer—John on the Isle of Patmos? Note the way John describes the same scene in the Revelation that David describes in Psalm 110.

> Then I saw heaven opened, and behold, a white horse. And He who sat on him was called Faithful and True, and *in righteousness He judges and makes war* (Rev. 19:11, emphasis added).

Trampling out the Vintage

It is in the words of Revelation 19:11–21 that we find the full exposition of the words of Psalm 110:2–3, 5–7. Not only do we say the King is coming but the *Judge* is coming, and He is coming to wage war. He does not come alone, for there is the large army of the redeemed who have "joyfully enlisted," who are in His great train: "And the armies in heaven, clothed in fine linen, white and clean, followed Him on white horses" (Rev. 19:14).

Psalm 110 speaks of the command to rule, the use of the rod of power, and the striking and smiting blows that will be necessary in that day. So John describes in verse 15:

> Now out of His mouth goes a sharp sword, that with it He should strike the nations. And He Himself will rule them

with a rod of iron. He Himself treads the winepress of the
fierceness and wrath of Almighty God.

Psalm 110 speaks of the battle as "the day of Your
power" (v. 3) and "the day of His wrath" (v. 5). John calls
it "the fierceness and wrath of Almighty God" (Rev.
19:15). And with the strong image of a vintner stomping
grapes, the splashing juice makes us think not only of
the first prophecy of this awful day in Joseph's words to
Judah, but also of a hymn we sing. The words of Joseph
were: "He washed his garments in wine, / And his
clothes in the blood of grapes" (Gen. 49:11). John says of
Jesus: "He was clothed with a robe dipped in blood" (Rev.
19:13).

And the hymn? It is, of course, the "Battle Hymn of
the Republic," which Julia Ward Howe clearly based on
the motif of Armageddon:

> Mine eyes have seen the glory
>   of the coming of the Lord,
> He is trampling out the vintage
>   where the grapes of wrath are stored;
> He hath loosed the fateful lightning
>   of His terrible swift sword–
> His truth is marching on.

The heaping of corpses (Ps. 110:6) serves as the setting
for the ghastly invitation to the carrion eaters to gorge
themselves on the flesh of the fallen (see Rev. 19:17–18).
The beast and his prophet, together with their allies, are
altogether defeated. The beast and the false prophet are
thrown alive into the lake of fire (see v. 20). The re-
mainder are killed (after He has refreshed Himself at
the brook?), and the birds are filled with their flesh.

No Fancy

Many people feel that Armageddon is a biblical scare
word, a Christian boogeyman. Passages such as Psalm

110 and Revelation 19 are often dismissed from the realm of reality because of the figurative language (e.g., "His eyes were like a flame of fire," Rev. 19:12). Once we get past the figures of speech, however, we may have an even stronger inclination to dismiss this concept. For—if we really think about it—the prospect of destruction and devastation these passages present is unthinkable!

Recently I was speaking in a prophetic conference in southern California on these themes. After one presentation, an obviously distressed woman came up to me and said, "I don't like that! I *really* don't like that!"

If this is your response, then the message has been presented fairly. We are *not supposed* to like God's judgment, either on ourselves or on others. The only things we may take satisfaction in are that when God judges, He does so out of the excellence of His character, and the result will be an end to deception. The final battle may not strike our fancy, but this will not be the first time that the God of glory does something without asking our permission!

Balaam's Song

Not only does the reality of these words not depend on our approval, but the teaching of final judgment is not a new truth in the song of Psalm 110. It is a truth that finds its origins in a text far more unlikely than this ancient song of glory. It goes all the way back to the improbable prophet Balaam, the pagan from Mesopotamia.

The story of Balaam is told in Numbers 22–24, 31. In Balaam we have one of the most surprising figures in the record of God's self-disclosure. This contemporary of Moses was not a believer in Yahweh the God of Israel in a saving sense, nor was he a friend of Israel in a covenantal sense. He came into the pages of Scripture to curse the people of God, but he became an unwilling means of bringing Israel great blessing instead. In the process he became an object lesson in the workings of the Abrahamic covenant.[10]

Despite all of the mystery concerning Balaam, we find that God spoke through him in a marvelous way. The prophecies of Balaam are in a cluster of seven oracles. The fourth of these prophecies is the most significant in terms of the far-reaching vista it presents. These are the words that Balaam uses to introduce his message:

> Then he took up his oracle and said:
> "The utterance of Balaam
>   the son of Beor,
> And the utterance of the man
>   whose eyes are opened;
> The utterance of him
>   who hears the words of God,
> And knows the knowledge
>   of the Most High,
> Who sees the vision of the Almighty,
> Who falls down,
>   with eyes opened wide" (Num. 24:15–16).

In these seven elements of introduction Balaam not only provides a solemn setting for his magnificent prophecy, he also reminds us of his pagan pedigree. After a lifetime of deception and involvement in demonic activities, he has confronted the God of reality. Balaam now has his eyes opened, has heard the very words of God. Then he presents his words.

This prophecy, which is set in the end time ("in the latter days," Num. 24:14), speaks of the very things we have seen in Psalm 110:2–3, 5–7. Hear the words of the prophecy:

---

[10]I do not have space here to develop these assessments. I have presented these issues, though, in the Feinberg *Festschrift* in my essay, "The Theology of the Balaam Oracles," pp. 79–119.

"I see Him, but not now;
I behold Him, but not near;
A Star shall come out of Jacob;
A Scepter shall rise out of Israel,
And batter the brow of Moab,
And destroy all the sons of tumult.
And Edom shall be a possession;
Seir also, his enemies,
   shall be a possession,
While Israel does valiantly.
Out of Jacob One shall have dominion,
And destroy the remains of the city" (vv. 17–19).

Balaam's prophecy of the distant future ("but not now" . . . "but not near," v. 17), speaks in a formal and solemn manner of a great figure who will arise from Judah one day and be the final victor over all his enemies. In the great battle he will be accompanied by his people ("Israel does valiantly," v. 18). He will be Star and Scepter. He will crush and destroy all of the foes before Him.

If you were to take the text of Numbers 24:15–19 and lay it down beside Psalm 110, I believe you would find that the same events are predicted and that they are also the same events described in Revelation 19. This means that the picture of the final and terrible battle of Armageddon was part of the earliest revelation to Israel, albeit through a strange means in the prophet Balaam.

And today, three-and-one-half millennia later, we read these words and find them to be still future. That Israel was told these things so long ago is remarkable. It is even more remarkable when we see that the first to sing the song of the Lord's battle cry of glory was Balaam.

And So We Sing

Psalm 110 is likely one of the most profoundly prophetic passages in all the Old Testament. Within these brief verses we are confronted with three great truths: (1) Jesus is the awaiting King; (2) Jesus is the eternal Priest; (3) Jesus is the avenging Judge.

Reading these words stirs us to join in *the hymn to His great glory:*

> Crown the Saviour, angels crown him!
> Rich the trophies Jesus brings;
> In the seat of power enthrone him,
> While the vault of heaven rings;
> Crown him! Crown him!
> Crown him! Crown him!
> Crown the Saviour King of kings.
>
> —Thomas Kelly

While the Buddha slumbers on yet in his grave, the Savior sits in active reigning majesty and in compassionate intercession. Leave the Buddha to sleep on! The King is coming. Julia Ward Howe said that her eyes had seen the glory of the coming of the Lord. In a way far more profound than she may have imagined, David *did* see the glory of the coming of the Lord.

Through the words of Psalm 110, so can we.

CHAPTER 11

A Troubled Song of Joy

Psalm 97

Fling wide your portals, Zion
  And hail your glorious King;
His tidings of salvation
  To every people bring,
Who, waiting still in sadness,
Would sing his praise with gladness.

—Frans Mikael Franzén, 1772–1847

In our study of the prophetic Psalms we have sung the songs of the triumphant battle of our Lord in the future campaign of Armageddon. Now we come to Psalm 97, and we are on the very horizon of the glorious reign of Zion's King.

At this future point the kingdom has been won, the protracted events of conflict have come nearly to a close, and the Lord Jesus Christ is now on His throne. In this prophetic vision in the hymns of ancient Israel, we may wonder what the immediate effects will be. They turn out to be two: *delight* and *devastation*. There will be delight among God's people, but devastation among those who do not know Him.

In our study of Psalm 2 we have seen the forces of evil gathering to challenge our Lord's right to rule. Then in Psalm 110 we witnessed the awful carnage of the battle itself. Now in Psalm 97 we have before us a song of the

joy of the righteous, troubled by the distress of the vanquished.[1]

Counterpoint of Mood

There is a counterpoint of mood in Psalm 97 that is a
distinctive artistic device. Hebrew poetry is based on
parallelism, a balancing of ideas and statements. One
line plays against another, and the combined effect gives
a deeper impression than either line alone can.[2] Psalm
97 uses these regular devices, but it also uses a disparity
of mood to heighten the effect of the song. Despair min-
gles with delight; both of these moods play against one
another in this poem.

As we often find in the briefer poems of the Psalter,
Psalm 97 has three movements: (1) verses 1–6, (2) verses
7–9, and (3) verses 10–12.

In the first movement of the poem we find that *the
reign of King Jesus will manifest itself in an awful display of His majesty.* In this description I am deliberately
using the word "awful" with a double intent: (1) to the
righteous, His majesty will be awe-provoking; but (2) to
the wicked it will be repulsive and condemning.[3]

The poem begins with these majestic words:

---

[1]Our arrangement of the sequence of the Psalms is artificial in this
discussion, of course. The poems themselves are not grouped chrono-
logically in the Psalter, but there is a clustering of several Royal
Psalms in the 90s (Psalms 93, 96–99).

[2]On the nature of parallelism in Hebrew poetry, see the writer's
Praise! A Matter of Life and Breath (Nashville: Nelson, 1980), Chapter
4, pp. 41–56.

[3]The word "awful," in the sense of "full of awe" or "awe-provoking,"
is well-attested among the older English writers. For example, King
Richard II, miffed at Northumberland for not showing deference, said:
"We are amazed; and thus long have we stood / To watch the fearful
bending of thy knee,/ Because we thought ourself thy lawful king:/
And if we be, how dare thy joints forget / To pay their *awful* duty to our
presence?" Shakespeare, *King Richard the Second,* act 3, scene 3, lines
72–76.

The LORD reigns;
Let the earth rejoice;
Let the multitude of isles be glad! (Ps. 97:1).

Here we have the delight of God's people in the fact that the Lord finally has assumed His reign. We enter into verse one with a comprehensive feeling of rejoicing, as the parallelism in the verse speaks of the whole (the earth) and the constituent parts (the multitude of islands) rejoicing together before the reign of the great King Jesus. That is, every part of the earth will have a people ready to praise the Savior on His return—the entire world, including the many islands and distant shores.

A Spinning Globe

One grade-school teacher who had a profound influence on my life once asked each child to come to her desk to select a country for a geography report. I remember spinning the world globe and watching it slow down. Then I put my finger on the island of Borneo! I could think of nothing more remote, exotic, or bizarre than that.

After we selected our topics and were ready to plagiarize from the encyclopedias, we heard our teacher say two things: "As you study this country," she said, "you might have in the back of your mind that some day you may visit there." Then she added (for she was a Christian teacher in a church school), "In any event, pray that God will establish His church in that country, so that when Jesus comes those people will be able to join the believers of the rest of the world in great joy." I do not know if her fine world view came from Psalm 97 or not, but she certainly had the spirit of verse one. Every constituent part of the earth is to join in our joy at the return of our Lord.

When our family planned for our sabbatical experience in Asia a few years ago, I thought, "Wouldn't it be something finally to go to Borneo after all of these years!"—wistful words.

Yet our great Father was working out some plans of His own! For God provided the ministry and the means for me to go to that part of the world. In an extraordinarily convoluted series of events which I alluded to in Chapter 7, I found myself in Surukum, Kalimantan Barat, Indonesia—the island of Borneo!

More wonderful to me than being in that exotic land—the realization of a childhood dream—was for me to be able to observe that God *was* building His church there. Those believers in that part of Indonesia will rejoice with believers everywhere when Jesus comes. All of the earth—and each of its parts—will be caught up in great rejoicing at the advent of our Lord. These are the exciting words of verse one.

Thick Clouds

Although Psalm 97 begins with the great joy that will come from all over the earth at the beginning of the reign of King Jesus, the mood changes in verses 2–5:

> Clouds and darkness surround Him;
> Righteousness and justice are the foundation of His throne.
> A fire goes before Him,
> And burns up His enemies round about.
> His lightnings light the world;
> The earth sees and trembles.
> The mountains melt like wax at the presence of the LORD,
> At the presence of the Lord of the whole earth (Ps. 97:2–5).

With the words "clouds and darkness" we have come to a context of judgment, no matter how unexpectedly. These words regularly portend judgment (see Joel 2:2; Zeph. 1:15; Ps. 18:11). All at once the light and happy sounds of verse one are contrasted with the dark and ominous sounds of verse two.

The deep clouds that descend on the throne of the living Christ in Psalm 97 are reminiscent of the poetic images used about Baal, god of storm and rain in Canaanite religion. The poets of the Bible made rich use of Baal mythology. Yet, in their use of the imagery, the Hebrew poets never adopted the theology of the pagan peoples in whose world they lived.

Baal was regarded by the Canaanite peoples as a god of rain and storm. When the rain was beneficent, then the clouds associated with him were clouds of blessing. But when the storm was destructive, then the image was fearsome.

One of the pictorial representations of Baal that has been discovered is a stela (an image in relief) from Ugarit (modern Ras Shamra), called by some the "Baal of Lightning."[4] In this image Baal's left hand is holding a lightning bolt that tapers into the shape of a spear. In his right hand is a war club or mallet. By casting the spear of lightning and beating on the drums of the heavens, he sent lightning and thunder to the earth. Then the storm god mounted his chariot and drove the clouds as a cowboy might drive cattle. Then he would bring rain—or so the story went.

For these reasons, this god was often associated with clouds and lightning.

In some of the poems of the Bible this type of language is used by God, not to reduce God the Almighty to the level of a pagan myth, but to magnify His works in exalted, figurative language. In the process, the Hebrew

---

[4]This stela has been reproduced often. The reader may find a picture of it in James B. Pritchard, *The Ancient Near East: An Anthology of Texts and Pictures* (Princeton: Princeton University Press, 1971), plate 136, where this image is dated 1900–1750 B.C. It is also found in the fiftieth anniversary volume on Ugarit by Gabriel Saadé, *Ougarit: Métropole Cananéenne* (Beirut: 1979), p. 134.

writers felt a strong sense of polemics; for if Yahweh was truly the God of storm and life and reality, then there was no room for Baal or his companions.

These images from the ancient world have come into our modern hymns as well. In the hymn "O Worship the King," Sir Robert H. Grant demonstrated a similar use of imagery:

> O tell of His might,
> O sing of His grace,
>   Whose robe is the light,
>   Whose canopy space.
> His chariots of wrath
>   the deep thunder clouds form,
> And dark is His path
>   on the wings of the storm.

As our poet describes the eclipse of the throne of the Lord which is being enveloped in storm-threatening darkness, we see that this is not a cover-up because of evil deeds. The throne that is being obscured is supported by righteousness and judgment, or righteous judgment.

Then from the center of the darkened throne flash forth searching, searing bolts of devastating lightning. Were this poem written in the twentieth century, perhaps the poet might have spoken of missiles or lasers. But in this early poem he speaks of lightning bolts which flash and spark and devastate all enemies, wherever they might be. A mountain refuge will not suffice against the heat of these missiles of judgment, for "mountains melt like wax" (v. 5) as the King executes justice.

On May 18, 1980, I was preaching on the doctrine of the coming judgment at a church in Oregon. After the service a young woman rushed up to me and said, "You know what you said about mountains melting like wax? Well, it has just happened! Mount St. Helens has just exploded!" Yet, as ruinous as the eruption of "our" volcano was, that eruption was just another Fourth of July cherry bomb compared to what is to come. As the old spiritual has it, "My Lord, what a mornin', when the stars begin to fall!"

"But isn't this just figurative language—this talk of lightning bolts and melting mountains?" Sure it is! But as we have seen before, figurative language in the Bible is figurative of *reality*. The reason the poets use such images is not to lead us to shrug their visions away, but rather to heighten our perception of the realities they are presenting. So the dark clouds, the bright lights, the noise and heat and searing bolts—all work together to give us a deeply felt perception of the reality of the coming judgment.

He Is Lord

Further, we should not miss the emphasis that Psalm 97 places on the identity of the source of the judgment which it so pictorially describes. It is from the LORD. As we have observed before, the Hebrew word underlying the English term LORD (all in capitals) is the name Yahweh. This is the personal name of God, which describes His essence as well as His ongoing relatedness to His people.[5]

In verse five the personal name Yahweh is balanced by the descriptive name "Lord" (note the lower case letters). The Hebrew word for Lord *(Adonai)* speaks of God as the supreme Master. He is the One in charge. The wording of Psalm 97:5 reminds me of Psalm 114:7, where the earth is called to writhe before the presence of the Lord *(Adonai),* before the One who is the God of Jacob (i.e., Yahweh).

---

[5]I have developed the meaning of the name Yahweh as revealed in Exodus 3 in my article, "What Is in a Name?" in William F. Kerr, *God: What Is He Like?* (Wheaton: Tyndale, 1977), pp. 107–127.

Once the awful judgment has run its course, the restatement of joy in verse six reminds us of the joy at the beginning of the poem:

> The heavens declare His righteousness,
> And all the peoples see His glory (Ps. 97:6).

This last verse of the first strophe serves with verse one as a frame of joy around the central picture of judgment. This is what I noted earlier in speaking of the interplay of mood within this Psalm. This is a *troubled* Psalm of *joy*. The joy of the redeemed is contrasted with the agony of the rebellious peoples who await God's judgment.

Now the joy of the righteous comes in knowing that wickedness will be at an end, a cleansing has been accomplished, the righteousness and glory of God are fully manifested, and the universe itself is affected. Now, at last, God's will *will* be done on earth as it is in heaven.

Now, at last, the ideals of the divine rule will be manifested fully and purely. Psalm 19 speaks of God's present revelation of His power and majesty through the universe He has made (vv. 1–6).[6] Psalm 97 speaks of the future revelation of God's righteousness and glory through the universe He has cleansed (v. 6). All of us are aware of the general lack of appreciation for God's ongoing revelation in nature today (see Rom. 1:18–23). In the coming revelation God will receive His intended response from all creation.

Awesome Destruction

In the first movement of Psalm 97 we have observed that the revelation of King Jesus will manifest itself in an awe-ful display of His majesty. There will be those

---

[6]See *Praise!*, pp. 129–149, for a development of Psalm 19.

who will respond to Him in great joy and awe; there will also be those who will be terrified of Him and will have to face the fury of His wrath. In the second movement of Psalm 97 we see that *the reign of King Jesus will provide an awesome destruction of all pretenders to His throne.* These are the verses in this section:

> Let all be put to shame
>   who serve carved images,
> Who boast of idols.
> Worship Him, all you gods.
> Zion hears and is glad,
> And the daughters of Judah rejoice
> Because of Your judgments, O LORD.
> For You, LORD, are most high above all the earth;
> You are exalted far above all gods (Ps. 97:7–9).

The world in which we presently live is a world besodden with idols, although some of us are slow to realize this. By studious ridicule and majestic praise, our Psalm speaks with rejoicing at the end of all idols. The poet speaks of those who "serve" idols, a verb that is regularly used in the proper service and worship of the true God (e.g., Ex. 3:12; 4:23). The second colon of verse seven adds the verb "to boast" to the verb "to serve." This is the dominant word for praise in the Book of Psalms. Here it is not used to describe the joyful boasting that the pious find in the Lord; it is used in a sarcastic manner to describe the impious who are involved in vainglorious boasting in worthless gods.

In our reading of the Bible we may come to feel that the subject of idolatry is wearisome. We have a general idea of what idols were in the ancient world, and we often think of them as something long ago and far away.

Idols, we understand, were images of false deities that flourished in the polytheistic thought of the primitive world, a world which we are well done with.

I sometimes find myself speaking of idols as things

used long ago by a people who lived in lands far away. In travels in the Holy Land, for example, one may observe today many relics of most unholy practices from the ancient world.

Megiddo

Think of Megiddo, that stunning tel that commands the Valley of the Jezreel and the word from which we get the name Armageddon. More than twenty layers of civilization have been exposed by archaeological cuts made on that site. It can be likened to a marvelously complex layer cake. Far below the level on which one stands today, in the Early Bronze Age level of the city, a flight of steps leads up to a large circular platform made of stones. Because of the accretion of the millennia, one looks *down* to see the top of this platform which, when it was first built, commanded a view of the valley below.

I have taken students down to the ancient stone platform and have recounted the prophetic indictments against idol worship that was done at such high places in periods of Israel's declension. Pagan rites and idolatrous worship took place on sites such as this. Our presence helped a bit to take away the "long ago and far away" feeling we usually have about idolatry. It helps to see an idol or a site of worship.

Among the genuine antiquities I have brought home from Israel are a few museum replicas of pieces that are too precious for me to own. One is an Astarte figurine. This clay idol is about six inches high. It was believed to be a goddess of sex and war.

This is the only piece that I have broken. A friend has told me that this piece was broken because I should not have it! He may be right. Even when I show this little nude deity in class to make more palpable the issue of idolatry in the ancient world, I sense that such concepts still remain something long ago and far away.

Idols Today

For this reason I am particularly grateful to the Lord for the opportunity He gave to our family to be in the Republic of China on our sabbatical a few years ago. While we were there we visited quite a few religious shrines of differing types. We confronted idol worship as it is being done *today*.

In November of 1978 we visited the temple of the goddess of the sea in the town of Peikang in the central part of the island of Taiwan. It was a high festival day; thousands of people had come to this little town to worship at this shrine. At one point we found ourselves tightly crowded together as we entered the building. On my left was my wife, Beverly. On my right was an elderly Taiwanese lady, her sleeveless shoulder pressed tightly against my bare lower arm. I *felt* her prayers. Her body trembled, her frame was so caught up in the intensity of her prayer. All this sincerity and urgency was directed to a god we know does not exist.

Then this woman cast her divination blocks to the ground. These blocks, made of wood or of bamboo root, are known variously as *poe* or *Bei*. They are shaped like a crescent moon. There are two of them, each a mirror image of the other. Both are flat on one side and round on the other. By the way that these *poe* would land on the ground, the woman would receive the response from her god to her prayer. Had these *poe* landed both flat side down, the answer from her god would have been an angry no. Had they landed one flat side down and one rocking on the rounded side, then her god would have been saying yes to her prayer.

As it turned out, both stones landed rounded sides down. Both were rocking—her god was laughing at her. As I watched her face, a solitary tear made its way down one of her wrinkled cheeks. Then she slunk down, turned, and made her way through the crowd to the outside.

It is my understanding that usually the negative *poe* is not taken so seriously, that there is a trick in the asking of the questions so that the desired response would finally come.[7] But in the case of this dear woman, the response she received from her supposed god seemed to be taken very seriously. If our thoughts go back to the laughter of God in Psalm 2 (see Chapter 9), we should remember that His scornful laugh was at His enemies, not at those earnestly praying to Him for help. In this case, a supposed god was thought to be laughing at one of his/her (?) friends!

No longer was the practice of idolatry something long ago and far away. I was crowded in and pressed about by all manner of living idolaters. In some parts of the world the practice of idolatry is still very real and omnipresent.

But in saying that idolatry is omnipresent in some lands, we do not suggest that a god of the imagination is omnipresent. Far from it! As we were still in that temple we saw a commotion off to our left. Aged priests were struggling to carry a ladder and then to right it. Then one priest made his way up the ladder and gave a "one-two" to a huge gong, high overhead.

Our missionary friend explained that she had seen a roll of bills pass from a young well-dressed man to one of the priests. Doubtless this man had come from another village, and he now wished to pray to his god. By having the brass gong sounded, he hoped to attract the attention of his god to this temple so that he might pray to him here. This man had no assurance that his god would hear, or that even if he/she were to hear, the god would respond.

---

[7]The practice of casting *poe* is discussed in a fascinating book by David K. Jordan, *Gods, Ghosts, and Ancestors: The Folk Religion of a Taiwanese Village* (Berkeley: University Press, n.d.), pp. 61–63. Incontrovertible is my major point: traditional Taiwanese people live in a world filled with many gods; idols abound in that little land.

Talk about Elijah on Mount Carmel! Do you recall the ribald attacks made on the false god Baal by the prophet of the Lord in his confrontation with the false prophets and priests on Mount Carmel? "Cry aloud, for he is a god; either he is meditating, or he is busy, or he is on a journey, or perhaps he is sleeping and must be awakened" (1 Kin. 18:27).[8]

In Taiwan we watched a man as hapless as those prophets of Baal whom Elijah mocked. He had to summon his god from another occupation, or at least try to do so. Idolatry is a very real phenomenon in our day. And our Psalm points to a day in which all idolatry will be put to shame.

Shame!

Of course idolatry is common in North America as well. One does not have to go to Israel and look at ancient sites of pagan rituals, nor does one have to go to Taiwan and watch villagers in their mantic acts.

After all, all that an idol is is a substitute for the living God. Substitutes for God do not have to be gross and repulsive. They may be pleasing and alluring. They may even be the "good things" of life—high-tech electronics, soap operas, fine food, Sunday football, chestnuts roasting by the fire. Even good things, if they take the place of God, become idols as surely as a carved image set in a niche.

All idols—and their adherents—will be judged at the second coming of Christ. Those in our culture who cling to false gods await a pronouncement of shame no less severe than that which shall come to the rankest primitive idolater.

"Let all be put to shame"! (v. 7). Imagine the force of

---

[8]The very ribald nature of Elijah's attack is given in The Living Bible translation of these verses.

the word "shame" if God is the speaker, and if the one
who hears this word has appeared before Him without
excuse. What a dreadful word that will be! "Shame!"
Perhaps this will be the last and only word that one will
ever hear from God. All of eternity will resound with
that awful word.

Nothingness

The words used concerning idols in Psalm 97:7 com-
bine together to present a picture of scathing denuncia-
tion. Here is a personal translation of this verse:

> They will be put to shame,
>   all those who serve graven images,
>   who boast themselves in idols;
> Prostrate yourselves before Him,
>   all you "gods"!

Three words are used for idols. The first term, "graven
image" (*pesel*), speaks of the origin of such gods. These
gods are made by the mind and imagination of man,
then are shaped by his hands. Isaiah 44 presents a
strong attack on such foolishness:

> Those who make a graven image,
>   all of them are useless,
> And their precious things shall not profit;
> They are their own witnesses;
> They neither see nor know,
>   that they may be ashamed (Is. 44:9).

The second term for idols in Psalm 97:7 is a
"bodacious" pun on the word for God in the Hebrew Bible, the word "Elohim." The Hebrew term Elohim is a
word that usually describes God in an intensive spelling
of the singular word *'el* (or *'eloah*). The basic meaning of
this word for God is likely the word "mighty." For this

reason, the intensive spelling Elohim, when referring to the true God, points to His unsurpassed might and worth. He is the Most Mighty. What a fitting term for deity in the story of creation (Gen. 1:1).

The word referring to idols in Psalm 97:7 is the Hebrew word *'elîlîm,* a word which sounds very much like the word for God. But this word is an intensive plural of the word *'elîl,* a word meaning "nothing"! That is, the gods of the nations are multiples of nothing. They are zip times zap. They are nothingnesses!

Fall Down before Him

When one has a substitute for God, he does not harmlessly cleave to something that is not quite as good as God. One without God is without good at all. He is without excuse (see Rom. 1:20), is deserving of God's wrath (see Rom. 1:21–32), is without hope (see Eph. 2:12), and awaits shame before the God he does not know (see Ps. 97:7).

We read in the last colon of verse seven that all of the supposed gods (*'elôhîm,* used in a sarcastic sense) will one day be broken in submission before Yahweh, as was the image of Dagon in the presence of the Ark of the Covenant (see 1 Sam. 5:1–5).

And to their devotees, no matter how sincere or well-meaning they might be, shall come the word of the living God: "Shame!" What an awful word that will be.

In verses 8–9 of Psalm 97 we read of the rejoicing of God's people at the devastation of these pretenders to the throne of God. Certainly there cannot be joy at human suffering. But there may be joy in knowing that never again will idolatry disgrace the creation of God. At that time all will know and confess in joy:

> For You (alone) O Yahweh
> are the Most High over all the earth;

You are exceedingly exalted
above all (imaginary) gods!
(Ps. 97:9, personal translation).

All-Embracing Demands

The third movement of Psalm 97 presents the idea
that *the reign of King Jesus will make all-embracing
demands of righteousness and joy among His people.*
Here is the third strophe:

> You who love the LORD, hate evil!
> He preserves the souls of His saints;
> He delivers them out of the hand of the wicked.
> Light is sown for the righteous,
> And gladness for the upright in heart.
> Rejoice in the LORD, you righteous,
> And give thanks at the remembrance of
> His holy name (Ps. 97:10–12).

Someone who longs today for the righteous reign of
King Jesus and someone who will be living during that
future reign have a common pursuit—an all-embracing
hatred of that which is evil and an all-consuming delight
in the Person who is altogether good. Those who are set
apart for His righteous reign can do no other.

It seems likely that it is not just evil in general which
verse ten refers to in its command, "You who love the
LORD, hate evil!" Rather, a particular type of evil seems
to be demanded by the context of verses 7–9. This is the
particular evil of idolatry. We are to abhor evil in general, of course. But a special hatred—a spurning, a
loathing—is to be attached to the particular evil which
pretends to occupy the place of God in many lives. *The
evil* we are to hate is idolatry.

Because we are engaged in this holy and healthy
hatred, what are we to do? Certainly we are to rescue

fools from the folly of their own idolatry. When we realize how evil idolatry really is, we cannot but strive to be used by the Lord to witness to light in this darkened age.

As we are engaged in this healthy hatred of the evil of God-substitutes, we shall find ourselves protected by God from the wicked ones who cling perniciously to their evil thoughts.

The Sower Goes Forth

I find myself particularly moved by the imagery of the poet in verse eleven: light and joy are sown.

Imagine the great King dismounting His glorious throne for a moment. He takes off His regal crown and royal robes. Then, as we watch in amazement, he puts on the simple garb of a farmer. As we watch, He puts two bags of seed on His broad shoulders. One of these bags is labeled "Light" and the other is labeled "Joy."

Then the King-Sower walks about the earth, so recently the scene of scorching bolts of searing judgment, and He begins the process of refructifying the earth. This is a planting that will lead to the millennial blessing. But the first seeds that our Lord plants are Light and Joy. He plants Light because now the darkness of judgment is gone. He plants Joy because the devastation of judgment is over. Now is the time for singing.

Our Joy

And to all of us, to those who first heard the music of this Psalm during the temple period and to us who sing this hymn of hope today, come the final words of joy and praise:

> Rejoice in the LORD, you righteous,
> And give thanks at the remembrance of
> His holy name (Ps. 97:12).

The mention of "His holy name" demands the recognition of the Hebrew term for God, Yahweh. It is this name by which God demonstrated His character to Israel in the Old Testament period. It is in this name that the Lord has revealed His saving actions in the person of our Lord. For the name Jesus is the final fulfillment of the name Yahweh (see Matt. 1:21; Phil. 2:11).

The last verse of Psalm 97 instructs us to proclaim His name exultantly *today*. We have come full circle in the poetry of this Psalm. This troubled Psalm of joy ends in total joy. Verse 12 matches the mood of joy in verse one. Here is the way Frans Mikael Franzén put it in the final stanza of his hymn, "Prepare the Way, O Zion!"

> The throne which he ascended
>   Is fixed in heaven above;
> His everlasting kingdom
>   Is light and joy and love;
> Let us his praise be sounding
> For grace and peace abounding.

The Lord Jesus *has taken* His place on His heavenly throne. This we know from Psalm 110. The Lord Jesus *will take* His throne here on earth. This we are reminded by Psalm 97. In both cases, great joy will animate the people of the King. In both cases, *song will be new.*

Yet we need to do more than sing. For we all know far too many people who still do not know the Savior; people are all about us who know nothing of our joy or our song. Unless you and I have a part in proclaiming the holiness of the name of the Lord in their hearing, these ones *we know* may never sing the song of praise to the King. They may instead hear from Him the terrible word *shame.*

Our own singing of these songs of joy ought to be tinged with sadness, and our lives with action. *Song will be new when Jesus reigns! Song may be new today* in the lives of those who know the coming King as their present Savior.

So let us sing. So let us live.

Finale

Let the Heavens Ring with Sound!

"Sing praises to God, sing praises!
Sing praises to our King, sing praises!"

CHAPTER 12

And Now, the New Song

Psalm 47

He will be great,
  and will be called the Son of the Highest;
and the Lord God will give Him
  the throne of His father David.
And He will reign over the house of Jacob forever,
  and of His kingdom there will be no end
  (Luke 1:32–33).

—The Angel Gabriel

There were no video game arcades when I was a boy. Instead of spending my youth shooting asteroids and gobbling blinking things, I grew up at the business end of a trumpet.

I don't play much anymore, but I still love a parade. Horses, pretty girls, floats, and especially bands—I love it all. And pageants—I'm a sucker for a pageant. I stayed up most of the night watching the royal wedding of Prince Charles and Lady Diana. Even Dan Rather could not help but smile and say his oohs and ahhs as one sumptuous carriage followed another, with a riot of color, sound, and tradition.

One day a parade and pageant will come that will make even beautiful Lady Diana's wedding splendor appear like Cinderella's dowdiness in her flight from the prince after the stroke of midnight. For one day the Lord Jesus Christ will be crowned King of Kings and Lord of Lords. What a day that will be!

What a day of color! Of sound! Of pageantry! What a day of song and praise! And we shall sing and clap and shout. In this chapter we shall look forward to that day.

We shall look forward to that day by turning once more to the Psalms of ancient Israel. In this chapter we shall look at two Psalms. One of them, Psalm 47, exalts in the music of that great day. The other, Isaiah 12 (a Psalm!), gives us lyrics for the praise of the Savior-King who mounts His throne.

Born to Die, Born to Rule

The angelic announcement of the birth of our Lord contained two great messages. The child who was to be born to Mary was both the promised Savior and the anticipated King.

When the angel spoke to Joseph he emphasized the *saving* actions of the promised One in the words, "and you shall call His name JESUS, for He will save His people from their sins" (Matt. 1:21). All born of women die; but the One promised to blessed Mary was born uniquely to die, as He came expressly to provide salvation for His people (see 1 Pet. 1:18–21).

When the angel spoke to Mary, he emphasized the *royal* action of the promised One in the words cited at the beginning of this chapter:

He will be great, and will be called the Son of the Highest; and the Lord will give Him the throne of His father David. And He will reign over the house of Jacob forever, and of His kingdom there will be no end (Luke 1:32–33).

So the One who was born to die was also born to rule. He "who Himself bore our sins in His own body on the tree" (1 Pet. 2:24) is the same as He "who has gone into heaven and is at the right hand of God, angels and authorities and powers having been made subject to Him" (1 Pet. 3:22; cf. Ps. 110:1). From that high and exalted

place we expect that His glory will one day be revealed
(see 1 Pet. 4:13) and that He will assume the very throne
of David vouchsafed for Him by the angel Gabriel in the
power of the Holy Spirit. In Psalm 47 we have a prophetic poem which pictorially displays the consumma-
tion of the rule of Christ on David's throne.

Here Comes the Victor

Psalm 47 has two bold movements—each filled with
music, excitement, pageantry, and majesty. In the first
movement we read *a command to all peoples to acknowledge openly the victory of the great King* (vv. 1–4).

> Oh, clap your hands, all you peoples!
> Shout to God with the voice of triumph!
> For the LORD Most High is awesome;
> He is a great King over all the earth.
> He will subdue the peoples under us,
> And the nations under our feet.
> He will choose our inheritance for us,
> The excellence of Jacob whom He loves.

As you read these words, can you not *feel* the excitement and exuberance in them? Here are words of
strength and courage that mark the mood of victory
achieved. Here are words of bold praise and open delight
that are appropriate to greet the return of the great Victor. Yet, before we see in these words the fulfillment of
the prophecies of the triumph of the Lord's Christ, let us
first consider what these words might have meant to the
ones who first sang them.

Some scholars believe that in this and in similar
Psalms an exceedingly complex cultic act is presented.
This act is believed to have been borrowed from Babylon.
In this view Psalm 47 and others like it were used in the
temple period to reenact on earth the annual enthrone-
ment of Yahweh in heaven during the New Year festival.

The idea is that the king of Israel served as a representative of God and displayed a pantomime of a heavenly ritual. Scholars who argue for this point of view tend to translate the opening words of several of the Psalms we have studied (93, 97, and 99) not as "Yahweh reigns," but rather as "Yahweh has become King."[1]

In contrast to these popular theories, it is my belief that this Psalm is a prophetic proclamation of the final victory of King Jesus over all His foes. This victory follows the campaign of Armageddon, elements of which we have seen described in Psalms 2, 110, and 97. Then this great praise Psalm comes to the strong Victor.

At the same time, this song may well have been sung in Israel on many occasions not only as a prophetic hope, but as a testimonial to God as the mighty Victor in their history. After a great battle in which Israel was supreme and the people knew this supremacy was an act of God, Psalm 47 could have been sung in the praise of God as King and as the source of their victory.

Yet I believe that in these victory celebrations the people of Israel would declare their immediate victories to be seen in the context of the ultimate victory that is to come at the end of the ages. The king ruling at any point in time in which a great victory might be achieved would be a foreshadowing of the coming King; present triumph would be a prototype of final triumph.

You and I might relate to this Psalm in the very same way. In any great victory in our own experience in which we magnify the Lord as the ultimate power who has brought us the victory, we find ourselves in the line of continuity of the victory Psalms. Each deliverance that

---

[1]This view was popularized by Sigmund Mowinckel in his seminal work, *Psalmenstudien,* 6 vols. (Oslo: Dybwad, 1922–24). It has had many champions, including Walter G. Williams, "Liturgical Aspects in Enthronment Psalms," *Journal of Bible and Religion* 25 (1957), pp. 118–122. It has also had many critics. You may wish to see the assessment given by Roland K. Harrison, *Introduction to the Old Testament* (Grand Rapids: Eerdmans, 1969), pp. 993–996.

the Lord brings to His people, whether in Israel's past or in our present, is a victory that speaks of the coming victory when Christ will burst into the realm of men to be crowned King of Kings and Lord of Lords.

So when we read the words of this old hymn we experience the feeling of being "between worlds." The verbs that in verses 3 and 4 in the past spoke of the future ("He *will* subdue" and "He *will* choose"), in the future will speak of the past ("He *has* subdued" and "He *has* chosen"). God, who has brought one victory after another, will Himself bring the final victory in the person of the Lord Jesus. And in His final victory His people will sing a new song.

Hear again the words of the central shout:

> For the LORD Most High is awesome;
> He is a great King over all the earth (v. 2).

These words will be the central declaration made by God's people as they respond to the Lord Jesus after the battle is over, the smoke has cleared, and light and joy are newly sown for His people (see Ps. 97:11).

Fear the Lord

He is awesome! The word "awesome" has been so trivialized by current slang as almost to be meaningless. On one occasion when I said that the Lord was awesome, a young lady came up to me and said that perhaps I should speak of the Lord as being "mega-awesome"! Nevertheless, in this poem the word "awesome" is invested with a powerful meaning. The Hebrew word is a form of the word "to fear." Our King is the one who ought to be feared. He is the One who is awe-inspiring, fearsome, and terrible.

Popular culture has so cheapened its view of Christ as to make Him appear dull, lackluster, complacent, and compliant. If Christ is the Lion of the Tribe of Judah, popular culture has taken away His teeth. We even hear that Jesus is "nice." Gasp. I suspect that the term "nice" is the least likely designation for the Lord of glory. Lions are not nice; they are awesome. Aslan the lion in the C. S. Lewis classic, *The Lion, the Witch and the Wardrobe,* is described in this way: "He is not nice, but he is good."

Not nice, but merciful; not sentimental, but faithful; not complacent, but in command—these are valid descriptions of our Lord. The excellence of His character is expressed in love and choice. The land of Palestine, the land of promise, is described in this poem as "the excellence of Jacob." It is the inheritance of Israel and the center of the kingdom that Christ will establish over all the earth.

All peoples, as we have seen in Psalm 97:1, are commanded to acknowledge openly the victory of the great King. He is Lord and He is Victor. He is Yahweh, the supreme designation of personal Deity in the Old Testament. He is the Most High, a term used often in the poetry of the Bible when God is described as the sovereign over all nations. And He is King.

God Has Ascended

In the second movement of Psalm 47 we find the complementary command that *all peoples are to praise skillfully the coronation of the great King* (vv. 5–9).

> God has gone up with a shout,
> The LORD with the sound of a trumpet.
> Sing praises to God, sing praises!
> Sing praises to our King, sing praises!
> For God is the King of all the earth;
> Sing praises with understanding.
> God reigns over the nations;
> God sits on His holy throne.
> The princes of the people have gathered together,

The people of the God of Abraham.
For the shields of the earth belong to God;
He is greatly exalted.

How more stirring can language be than the words of
this poem? At verse five we read, "God has gone up." In
verse nine, "He is greatly exalted." The verbs in these
two expressions are from the same root: He has ascended
and now is exceedingly exalted. These words act as the
beautiful frame for the picture of the new song of praise
that marks His coronation.

As anticipated in the words of the first strophe
(vv. 1–4), the victory of the ages has been won in a wonderful manner. Whereas the rulers of the present darkness once were gathered together to attempt to block the
return of the Victor (see Ps. 2), now—in the prophetic
posture of this Psalm—the new leaders of the world are
gathered together as one great people. All nations and
all peoples are gathered together in the binding cords of
the Abrahamic covenant, for the blessing of all is to be
found only in the seed of Abraham (see Gen. 12:3). Gen-
tiles and Jews are now one people indeed, "the people of
the God of Abraham" (Ps. 47:9). All of their shields belong to the victor. They are hung on the trophy walls of
the new palace as a symbol of lasting victory. No longer
will weapons of warfare be needed; the Prince of Peace
has brought true *shalom.*

Let There Be Music

Read the words of the second movement again. Do you
see the tremendous emphasis upon *music*? There will be
clapping and shouting (v. 1), but it will be *music* that
will best adore the exalted glory of the King. The repeated words, "Sing praises!" are not redundant; they
are emphatic. Music is to adorn His crown and sparkle
on His robe. Let there be song!

The words of verse seven are particularly important

for us to linger over: "Sing praises with understanding." These words speak both of appropriateness in music as well as in the requisite skill of the players and singers. Great music becomes ordinary if performed poorly; the greater the music, the greater the demands upon the artist. It is very difficult for a young musician to play a well-known work. Comparisons are too easily made with great masters; the young only have a chance if they truly excel.

Musical skill lies not only in playing and singing, but also in selecting the appropriate music. Think again of the wedding of Prince Charles and Lady Diana—an experience shared by people all over the world. What would that wedding have been like without the bells of the English churches? Without the choirs? Without the bands and the orchestras? What if there had been *no* music? It would not have been the same wedding. Think of *any* wedding without music, and a festive occasion becomes somber and officious.

Now think of a royal wedding that has music, but the music is inappropriate. What if disco music had filled St. Paul's Cathedral on July 29, 1981, instead of the music of Handel? What if Elton John had been substituted for Edward Elgar and William Walton? Even fine music performed with skill will not suffice if the music itself is inappropriate for the occasion.

The music that will be performed and sung at the coronation of the King of glory will be both appropriate in its selection and skillful in its performance. Anything less would ruin the occasion.

And our music today? Ouch! How often have we been led to believe that whatever we do is all right—that it is good enough for church. "Good enough for God" is sometimes not good at all. In fact, only the best is really good enough.

There is a danger in stressing the art of music over the heart of the people worshiping the Lord with their singing. Yet those who have a heart for God cannot ignore art when they worship Him with music.[2]

Consider the music we sing today as praise offerings to the King in the context of worship music through the ages. From the Psalms of the Old Testament to the music at the coronation of the King, a *continuity of excellence* is always presented to God's people. God's demand in our music is simple. It is the same demand He makes in all of our life—excellence. We are to play and to sing *with skill* to His glory, both now and in the age to come.

On the Throne, at Last!

The central acclamation of the second part of Psalm 47 is found in verses six and seven: God reigns! Listen to these three lines again:

> God is the King of all the earth!
> God reigns over the nations!
> God sits on His holy throne!

These three synonymous declarations enhance our wonder and demand our praise in song. At last! There He is! Think of all the prayers that must have gone up to the Lord during the time of the temple worship, entreating Him who promised to rule with His people on earth to soon do it. "In our time, O Yahweh; in our time!" Such is the nature of prayer through the ages.

In the model prayer of our Lord, we have both a petition and an affirmation concerning the rule of God. The petition is in the words, "Your kingdom come" (Matt. 6:10). The affirmation is in the words, "For Yours is the kingdom" (Matt. 6:13). On one hand we pray for the coming of the kingdom of God to the earth, that the will of

---

[2]Gordon Borror and I have attempted to stress the delicate balance between art and heart in worship in our book, *Worship: Rediscovering the Missing Jewel* (Portland: Multnomah, 1982).

the King be done on earth even as it is presently done in heaven. On the other hand we acknowledge that God *is* King; He has always been King (see Ps. 93).

But how many saints through the ages have prayed, "Thy kingdom come"? And how many times have they prayed these words? And now, at last, in the prophetic stance of Psalm 47, these words have been answered. The Lord reigns!

Here we have the goal of history, the desire of the ages, the hope of time. The King has come. "Let heaven and nature sing!" And so let His people sing. Is there any wonder that at the coming of the Lord Jesus *song will be new*?

As you and I worship the Lord today in the world between, let us keep in mind the music that will one day come before His throne. I love the way that Nancy Spiegelberg calls for excellence in the adoration of God and a spurning of that which is ignoble and debasing. This is from her poem, "Good Taste."

> Bread of God
> train me not to
> ruin my appetite
> for You
> by filling up on the goodies
> and the trash
> of this world.[3]

The Good Song of Praise

Not only do I love the way Nancy Spiegelberg calls for excellence in our adoration of God today, but I also love even more the song that Isaiah wrote especially for the time of the coronation day of the Lord Jesus Christ. Psalm 47 calls for singing; Isaiah gives us the words.

---

[3]From Nancy Spiegelberg and Dorothy Purdy, *Fanfare: A Celebration of Belief* (Portland: Multnomah, 1981), p. 20. Used by permission.

In Chapter 1 we surveyed the opening chapters of Isaiah's great prophetic book. We may pause for a moment and rehearse the setting for the great Psalm of the kingdom that Isaiah presents in chapter 12.

After Isaiah gives the prophecy of the establishment of Jerusalem as the new center of worship, from which the Torah (the Law) will flow and in which peace will prevail (see 2:1–5), he then gives the music for the rule of the King. After he speaks of the prophecy of the holy Seed that is in the stump of the felled tree of the House of Jesse (see 6:13), Isaiah points to the song of the King. After Isaiah speaks of Immanuel (see 7:14), of the birth of the wonder Child who is the God-man (see 9:6–7), of the beautiful Branch from the stem of Jesse (see 11:1), Isaiah then gives us the song.

All of these prophecies and more lie behind the great hymnic text of Isaiah 12. This is a text which is specifically located in the coming day of the rule of the beautiful Branch, the Lord Jesus. Listen to the words and hear their music. *Here is the new song!* The song is in two parts, as is Psalm 47. The first movement reads:

> And in that day you will say:
> "O LORD, I will praise You;
> Though You were angry with me,
> Your anger is turned away,
>   and You comfort me.
> Behold, God is my salvation,
> I will trust and not be afraid;
> 'For YAH, the LORD,
>   is my strength and my song;
> He also has become my salvation'"
> Therefore with joy will you draw water
> From the wells of salvation (Is. 12:1–3).

Here is the response to Psalm 47: to sing praises to the King with skill and appropriateness. In this first movement we sense the wonder of praising the Lord who only recently was angry, but whose anger is now turned, and who has become His people's source of comfort.

The Surprise of God

What a surprise it is to find that the very God who had been angry is now the source of comfort! We may think on a personal level of the anger of God, which each of us deserves. But there in the darkness that hovered over the Holy City—for heaven blushed to see the sight—the One who knew no sin became "sin for us" (2 Cor. 5:21), and the anger of God we rightly deserve was deflected from us to His broad, but deeply bowed shoulders.

Each of us may sing the words of this Psalm of God's grace in praise to Him for what we presently know. What a surprise! *God* is our salvation! Our strong song is in Yah, the LORD (v. 2). In these words Isaiah has used both the short and the long forms of the name of God. The Hebrew may be read "Yah, Yahweh." It is as though in his excitement the poet believed that even the name of God by itself was insufficient to express his joy. He doubles the name as an expression of his praise.

While this Psalm may be sung by us today in our praise of God for the surprise of His grace, Isaiah specifically locates this Psalm "in that day." That is, this poem has its specific setting in the day when the King is on His throne, when sin is practiced no longer and men dwell in tranquility. This is the day when the changes in men are reflected by changes even in nature. Carnivores and herbivores will dwell together; predators will lie with their prey, and little children will be safe with vipers (see Is. 11:6–8). This is the day in which:

> They shall not hurt nor destroy
>   in all My holy mountain,
> For the earth shall be full
>   of the knowledge of the LORD
> As the waters cover the sea (Is. 11:9).

Sing Again

What a day that will be for song! Hear now the words of the second movement of Isaiah's hymn of the kingdom.

> And in that day you will say:
> "Praise the LORD, call upon His name;
> Declare His deeds among the peoples,
> Make mention that His name is exalted.
> Sing to the LORD,
> For He has done excellent things;
> This is known in all the earth.
> Cry out and shout,
> O inhabitant of Zion,
> For great is the Holy One of Israel in your midst!"
> (Is. 12:4–6).

As in the first movement, Isaiah signals the time for the singing of this song; "that day" is the day of the reign of the King of glory as depicted in the preceding chapter of his prophecy. It is the day of the singing of Psalm 47, but here are the words of the new song.

And what is the new song? It is the *old* song of God's wonder and grace sung with *new enthusiasm*. The new song is the song of praise, of public declaration, of the active recognition of His name. All of these elements fill the Psalms.

There is, however, a *new thing* in the new song. That which is genuinely new is not the fact that God is worthy of our praise. That which is new is that He has made His dwelling among His people. This poem, which ends in the words "great is the Holy One of Israel in your midst," points to that day when the Savior-King has ascended His throne, where He sits in regal majesty, the delight of all His people.

The first movement of this poem ends with words describing salvation as water in a well, plenteous and pure! For people in Judah, whose lives were so actively dependent upon the search for adequate water, such an image of salvation must have been stirring indeed. The point of these words is that the salvation God has provided is to be enjoyed.

In the second movement of the poem we find the emphasis not so much upon the salvation that God has provided as it is upon the Savior who has brought it. The first movement calls upon the people of God to enjoy their salvation; the second calls upon them to enjoy their Savior. The Holy One is now in the midst of His people. *This* is the essence of the new song.

Psalm 47 presents a dynamic picture of the Lord of glory seated on His throne, adored by His people in song. Isaiah 12 presents the song that will be sung in that day, a new song of praise to the Savior-King who dwells with His people.

While these songs speak of the future, we read them today. Since we read them today, we can sing them as well. What a day *that* will be for song! What a day *this* is for song! Today we sing in anticipation of His coming. We also sing in the realization of God's present rule in our lives.

The new song of the King can be new in our lives today. All we have to do is sing.

· CHAPTER 13 ·

So Let Us Sing!

Traue Gott! Sieh, er verziehet nicht lang.
Bitte Gott! Traue Gott! Sieh, er verziehet
  nicht lang.

Trust God! See, He tarries not long.
Pray to God! Trust God! See, He tarries
  not long.

> —Samuel Freidrich Sauther/
> Beethoven, "The Quail's Song"

Song will be new when Jesus the Savior comes to reign
on the earth as our great King-Priest. Yet song may be
new now in our lives as we live in the age of expectation.
The words of the Psalms call for a new song today, a song
of freshness, skill, and fervor—qualities that are often
lacking in the music of the church. Yet, here and there
we are delighted to find church musicians who are truly
fresh, genuinely skillful, and filled with fervor born of
the Holy Spirit. With them we find ourselves filled with
song.

Poetry Plus

Throughout this study of the prophetic Psalms we
have emphasized four main points.

The Psalms are poetry. This assertion means that
when we read the Psalms we should attempt to do more

than just analyze the words to determine facts. Along with our careful reading we should strive to share in the *experience* of these poems. In the poems we have studied we have laughed and winced, we have wept and wondered. We have read these poems well when we have *felt* with them.

The Psalms are worship music. For this reason we have read these poems as art, but not just as art for art's sake. We have sought to read these poems in a way that would inspire us to join together in the adoration of God, the thrice-holy King. In leading us to declare His works together, these old songs sing anew. They restore and refresh our singing.

The Psalms are relevant to life today. These poems make demands upon our life-style, just as they made demands upon those who first sung them thousands of years ago. The Psalms have the integrity of life about them. They do not pretend; they demand. These poems may not be ignored; they are to be lived.

The Psalms contain great prophecy. Not all the Psalms are prophetic, but some do contain significant prophecy concerning the first advent of our Lord and also His second coming. The prophecy they present is largely geared to shape our attitudes rather than answer our questions. The prophecy presents the King to be adored rather than a detailed program of prophetic chronology.

We may not have read any of these Psalms rightly if in our reading of them we have not reexamined who we are and where we are in our relation to God.

Even as I type these words I am listening to a recording of the Psalms set to splendid contemporary Jewish melodies. I am so moved by these words in their musical setting that my progress at this moment is slow and halting. And yet as I type on (for there is a deadline to meet!), I hurt inside; for it is my understanding that the composer who has set the wonderful words of life in the Psalms to new melodies, does not himself know the Lord of those words. What a puzzle! New songs, beautiful music, words of life—but no relationship to the Lord of the text.

And where are you, dear reader? Not all who have read the Psalms have really read them well.

New Song Today

So we believe that the Psalms of the coming of the King present a picture of a future time when song will be new as God's kingdom is revealed newly on this earth. These songs also present a call for new song in our lives today as we experience His present rule. The one who *is coming . . . has come.* As He makes His coming known in our lives, then song is new *now.*

When it comes to the subject of biblical prophecy, many people seem to have lost a sense of values. Some want to be the first on the block with a seven-year supply of dehydrated food. There are supply companies that presently advertise just for such people. Pop prophecy has become a fad.

How many more groups will there be who will listen to leaders who are "absolutely positive" that they have discovered the day of the translation of the church or of the return of the Lord? One sect in Arizona saw the day of the rapture come and go—twice—in 1981. According to a report distributed by the Associated Press (July 11, 1981), an earlier forecast for June 28 was revised to August 7. The new calculation was said by the leader of this sect to be "absolutely sure." "Truly," the leader is reported to have said, "this is the last forty days."

Well, back to the drawing boards! Both days came. Both days went. The Lord did not come on either of them. I have a friend who says that the one day the Lord will probably *not* come is the day that some Christian forecaster says is *the* day.

More recently there have been full-page ads appearing

in a large number of daily newspapers across America and in several other countries of the world suggesting strongly that the Lord Jesus Christ has already returned to the earth but is presently going about incognito. He will soon be revealing Himself, however. . . .

And a month comes, and a month goes. And we have lost the song.

I was in Tucson not long ago, and I heard a report on an art exhibit at the Pima County Fair. One picture received a considerable amount of attention. A film crew from a local television station set up its equipment near the painting and asked questions of passers-by. Comments recorded on film for the evening news concerning this painting ranged from "thoughtful" to "mysterious and gripping" to "beautiful." One art teacher spoke of the "delicate balance and control of the artist." Another rhapsodized on the "shadow and contrast, delicately balanced." Another said, "a true original." If nothing else, I learned a fine set of comments to make about the next painting I see.

And the painting over which these ebullient words were given? It was a prank. A well-known artist had submitted an absolutely blank canvas with a beautiful frame. There it hung in a place of honor, well-lighted, centrally displayed. And nearby was the film crew.

Where is the child who will finally say, "But the emperor has no clothes on!" Where is the person who will remark concerning the silliness and pettiness that seem to characterize so much of the current interest in biblical prophecy—"But, where is the music?"

Let Us Sing

Song will animate the kingdom of Christ the Lord. Song should fill our lives today as we recognize the rule of the King. Here are some ways that we can maintain a fresh and vital song in these troubled days.

Song will be new among God's people as we focus our attention on the Person of our King.

Note the reasons given for the song in the Book of the Revelation:

> And they sang *a new song,* saying:
> "You are worthy to take the scroll,
> And to open its seals;
> For You were slain,
> And have redeemed us to God
> by Your blood
> Out of every tribe and tongue
> and people and nation,
> And have made us kings and priests
> to our God;
> And we shall reign on the earth" (Rev. 5:9–10,
> emphasis added).

That which sets the creatures and elders of heaven into singing a new song is the contemplation of the Lamb who is worthy. When our affections are upon Him, we can then sing.

Song will be new among God's people when we have in our midst people who are singing anew.

The call for a new song in the Book of Psalms is not just a call for a new hymnal or a new song leader. It is a call for a new sense of reality of the presence of the great King among His people. We tend to develop such an appreciation when we are around people who themselves are singing.

Singers beget singing. Worshipers beget worship. Music is infectious. Singing in the Psalms is a corporate act. The commands to sing in the Psalms are regularly in the plural (e.g., Ps. 98:1). We shall sing the new song more readily if we are with people who themselves are new to the song or have learned another stanza.

We have friends who have been serving the Lord in Papua New Guinea. They have recently met with some of the village leaders concerning the distribution of the New Testament that is now in the national language and ready for use. Roger Garland asked the tribal leaders what kind of a celebration they might like to have. According to his personal letter, here is the response that Roger received:

> One of the men, Bana, stood up and asked, "How long have you worked on this?" Roger replied, "Oh, about ten years." Bana then held up the New Testament and said, "When we finished the new clinic we had a big celebration and that only took three months to build. That clinic is only for our bodies, but this is for our souls. I think we should have a big day to celebrate." And with these words all the village leaders agreed.

"Oh, about ten years!" A decade of life was glossed over in these words! Roger, Susan, and their boys had lived in the jungles of New Guinea for ten years to achieve this day. Did they sing? They did indeed. How could they not sing in such a setting—a newly forming community of God and the newly translated Word of God?

Song will be new among God's people as we keep alert to the activities of the King in the world about us.

A year ago I was ministering in a church in southwest Minnesota. I learned that a little boy from a farm across the border in Iowa had wandered into the fields of corn that encircled his house. A massive search began that was to last for three days and was to involve thousands of people. They searched for him Thursday, Friday, and Saturday.

Night came on that Saturday. With it came a prevailing sense of gloom. The boy's parents stood on their back porch and thanked the people who had worked so hard. They had searched six miles square. The fields nearest the house had been searched five or six times each. But little Justin, only two-and-a-half, had not been found. The parents thanked the people for their prayers on behalf of their little boy. Then they commended their child to God and told the people not to return the next day.

The search was off.

But one farmer kept on looking. After all others had stopped, he kept on. Forty-five minutes after the search had been canceled, this intrepid farmer found Justin. The little boy was frightened and whimpering. He was dehydrated and covered with mosquito bites. He was taken to the hospital and was found to be sound and was released, sucking on a popsicle for moisture.

The next morning a film crew from the local television station filmed the morning worship service where the family gave praise to God in their community of faith. *And did they sing!* And in their joy in the work of the King in their midst, all who saw that broadcast later in the same day joined in the song. Song was made new in our hearts as we witnessed the grace of God in the response to countless prayers on behalf of a lost little boy.

Song will be new among God's people as we see new singers joined to the company of the redeemed.

Psalm 96 is a Royal Psalm that calls for a new song. In this lovely Psalm of world mission we are confronted with the imperative of evangelism in the context of the new song. Listen again to the opening words of this Psalm:

> Oh, sing to the LORD a new song!
> Sing to the LORD, all the earth.
> Sing to the LORD, bless His name;
> Proclaim the good news of His salvation
>   from day to day.
> Declare His glory among the nations,
> His wonders among all peoples (Ps. 96:1–3).

In these strong words that call repeatedly for music, there is also a magnificent appeal for worldwide response. "All the earth" is to join in the song. "All nations" are to hear of His glory and "all peoples" of His wonders.

"For He is coming, for He is coming to judge the earth"
(v. 13).

*Song will be new among God's people as we realize how
beautiful praise is to Him.*

One of the Psalms that calls for a new song stresses
the beauty of praise. Our audience in worship is not one
another; our audience is God. When He is praised truly,
it is an act of beauty. This is the message of the opening
movement of Psalm 33.

> Rejoice in the LORD,
>   O you righteous!
> For praise from the upright is *beautiful.*
> Praise the LORD with the harp;
> Make melody to Him with an
>   instrument of ten strings.
> Sing to Him a new song;
> Play skillfully with a shout of joy (Ps. 33:1–3, emphasis
>   added).

These words call for a new song of beauty, which will
be received by the King as an adornment to His majesty.

*Song will be new among God's people as we rehearse
His mercies on our behalf.*

This is certainly the sentiment of Psalm 40:1–3. In
this well-loved messianic hymn which speaks of the Incarnation of our Lord (vv. 6–8; cf. Heb. 10:5–10), there is
testimony to God's acts of deliverance that bring a new
song and lead to the salvation of many.

> I waited patiently for the LORD;
> And He inclined to me,
> And heard my cry.
> He also brought me up out of a horrible pit,
> Out of the miry clay,
> And set my feet upon a rock,
> And established my steps.
> He has put *a new song* in my mouth—
> Praise to our God;

Many will see it and fear,
And will trust in the LORD (Ps. 40:1–3, emphasis added).

There are those who say that they are not interested in using worship time for public testimony. They have either heard too many self-serving statements in the guise of testimony, or they have not listened to the imperatives of the Psalms. The redeemed are to say so—to the community. The delivered are to say so as well—to the community. Whom the Lord has delivered, let him sing a new song.

Song will be new among God's people when we recognize fully that the coming King is our present King.

Hear these words of David, in a wonderfully complex composition whose message is simple and direct, the opening words of Psalm 145:

> I will extol You, my God, O King;
> And I will bless Your name
>   forever and ever.
> Every day I will bless You,
> And I will praise Your name
>   forever and ever.
> Great is the LORD
>   and greatly to be praised;
> And His greatness is unsearchable (Ps. 145:1–3).

Here the new song of David is based on the recognition that the God of Israel is presently King. How can we sing the song of the King who is to come in an age that knows so much pain and suffering? We can do so when we recognize that the King who is to come is King today. He can be adored today. He can be served today. And His power is not limited, no matter how desperate our age.

Music, maestro! God is King! The King is coming! He is coming in the context of music. May our voices and our lives sing both today and *when song is new!*